Ala

Wildlife Viewing Guide

Exploring the Nome Roadways

Writers
Anne Sutton and Sue Steinacher, Alaska Department of Fish and Game (ADF&G)

Technical Contributors
Peter Bente, Tony Gorn, Jim Menard, and Kate Persons; ADF&G
Charlie Lean, Norton Sound Economic Development Corporation
Gay Sheffield, Marine Advisory Program, University of Alaska Fairbanks

Project Managers and Editors
Anne Sutton, Peter Bente, and Beth Peluso; ADF&G

Design, Layout, and Maps
Graphic Design/Map Design/Layout: Kim Mincer, Bureau of Land Management
GIS Maps: Sally Timp, ADF&G

Publisher
ADF&G/Division of Wildlife Conservation

Wildlife Viewing Program
P.O. Box 115526
Juneau, AK 99811
(907) 465-5157 (p)
(907)465-6142 (f)
dfg.dwc.hq-info@alaska.gov

Arctic and Western Regional Office
P.O. Box 1148
Nome, AK 99762
(907) 443-2271

Front cover photo: ©Tom Kohler - muskox
Back cover photos: ©Tom Kohler - moose, seal, and bluethroat
©Sue Steinacher - monkshood and ice fishing
©Riley Woodford - bear tracks.

CONTENTS

Nome Area Roads

INTRODUCTION

Welcome to the Seward Peninsula and a rare opportunity to explore the wildlife, landscapes, and lifestyles of Alaska's Arctic by road. Though gravel and maintained only seasonally, three main byways lead out of Nome and cover more than 250 miles of wild-lands. Here rocky surf-battered headlands share coastline with long sandy beaches, and coastal breezes ripple sheltered lagoons. Clear water streams tumble from glacially-carved mountains, rolling carpets of tundra harbor wildflowers and tiny berries, and precious few trees block the view.

A herd of reindeer finds it easier to travel by road than across the tussock tundra.

At various times during the last Ice Age, this land was part of the Bering Land Bridge (also called Beringia)—a roughly 1,000 mile wide swath of land that joined Siberia and mainland Alaska. Today's peninsula juts into the Bering Sea just below the Arctic Circle and the Chukchi Sea. Few people live in this remote location (Nome, pop. 3,600, is the region's largest community) but the discovery of gold near the turn of the last century fueled a brief but frenzied development that led to the construction of now defunct railroads and still-traveled roads.

Alaska's Nome Area Wildlife Viewing Guide will introduce you to the area's three major roads and the wildlife that you may see in summer: muskox or moose munching in willow thickets, brown bear roaming mountain slopes, curlews nesting in tundra, songbirds flitting in boreal forest, whales coursing through ocean waters, and salmon and grayling slipping over gravel streambeds. The people who live here are also an integral part of the landscape. Like visitors, they take pleasure in observing wildlife, but they also value having healthy, flavorful wild game and fish on the table and a fur ruff to protect against winter's bitter winds.

A fur ruff on a young girl's parka protects against winter's chill.

This guidebook points out possible wildlife viewing locations by milepost for each gravel road along with birding hot spots within walking distance in and around Nome. You will also find animal and habitat descriptions and a glimpse at the type of year-round animal and human activities that few visitors ever see.

Whether you are discovering the Seward Peninsula for the first time or know its crannies well, you may find this guidebook and a trip along the roadways will spark new ways of seeing and appreciating the interconnections of wildlife, people, and the land.

How to use this guidebook

This book is organized by habitat, species, and roadway location. Before you begin driving, familiarize yourself with the sections listed below. This will help you find information more easily in the field. Be sure to review the safety precautions and take appropriate safety equipment with you. You will find binoculars and a good field guide to birds to be useful companions to this guidebook.

I. Overview includes wildlife viewing and safety tips, a description of the Arctic seasons, and a calendar of wildlife and subsistence activities.

II. Wildlife Habitats describes the ten most common habitat types encountered along the road system and the animals and birds typically found there. If you familiarize yourself with this section, you'll have an idea of what to look for at any point along the way.

III. Wildlife Facts provides background on the life history and—in several cases—the management history of some of the more viewable mammals and fish.

IV. Milepost to Roads lists a number of locations along the three main roads and the wildlife most likely to be seen there. It is impossible to pinpoint specific viewing opportunities, however, as wildlife ranges freely across broad expanses of land. Be aware that most outlying roads are closed in winter. This section also includes background information on road-accessible communities and cultural and historic sites, as well as a Nome walking tour for birders.

OVERVIEW

Wildlife Viewing Tips

Stop at river crossings and vantage points that offer broad views of various habitat types and scan the surrounding area. Even a short walk may open up new opportunities to see wildlife or signs of wildlife, such as a grizzly crossing a distant slope or tufts of **qiviut**—the soft underlayer of wool on muskox—caught in willow branches.

Look with binoculars or a spotting scope to improve your chances of finding wildlife. Polarized sunglasses that cut glare will enhance fish and other wildlife viewing in and around water and make for safer driving in the low-angled sun.

Listen whenever you stop and turn off your vehicle's engine. You will begin to discover the sounds and signs of birds and smaller animals surrounding you. If you do get out, pull the key so the door alarm doesn't sound and close the door gently or you may send nearby wildlife fleeing.

Binoculars make wildlife viewing much more rewarding.

Travel when the light is right. Consider altering your sleep schedule during the height of Nome's long mid-summer days. Many animals are more active during the low light of late night or early morning or at dawn and dusk other times of the year.

Look for changes in patterns. Familiarize yourself with the patterns and colors of vegetation, rocks, or water. Be alert for subtle changes that could reveal the presence of animals.

Know your wildlife. Feeding habits, seasonal movements, and preferred habitats are clues for where to look for wildlife. Be familiar with the major habitat types described in this guidebook.

Learn to "see" wildlife in other ways. Look for animal tracks in the wet sand at creek crossings or in the snow in winter. Listen for bird songs and calls to expand what you find.

Respect others. People enjoy wildlife for a variety of reasons. Many local people rely on wild game, fish, berries, and greens for food. Please do not interfere with hunting, fishing, or subsistence activities and respect others' viewing opportunities as well.

Safety Around Wildlife

People and wildlife often cross paths on the Seward Peninsula so it is important to understand basic wildlife safety principals. Our general guidelines are followed by advice on specific animals.

Animals need plenty of space. Use binoculars or spotting scopes in order to view animals from a distance without altering their behavior. Make your observations in a quiet and indirect manner to avoid disturbance. Always give them an avenue for retreat and never chase an animal.

Recognize signs of alarm or stress. Sometimes subtle, these vary among species but may include increased movements such as agitated flapping or pacing,

Young animals may appear to be alone but often have a parent nearby.

heightened muscle tension, staring, or frequent vocalizations. If you sense that an animal is disturbed by your presence, back off. Leave if it does not resume normal behavior.

Respect nesting, calving, and denning sites. Well-meaning but intrusive people may cause an animal parent to flee, leaving their young vulnerable to predators or the elements. Keep your distance and retreat if an animal shows signs of distress. Nesting birds are also sensitive to disturbance and being too close can impact nesting and cause other problems. Leave if birds flush and show alarm at your presence.

Leave "orphaned," sick, or wounded animals alone. If you want to report your concerns, see the Emergency Contacts section at the end of the book.

Feeding wildlife is dangerous for you and the animal. Feeding animals is illegal. It can make them dependent on handouts and lose their fear of people. Handouts can also harm their digestive systems.

Rabies may be present. Any mammal in this region can carry rabies although most cases locally involve canine species, especially foxes. Be wary if an approaching animal displays no fear, salivates heavily, or appears weak or paralyzed. If you are bitten by a wild animal, seek medical attention as soon as possible.

Pets can disturb wildlife. Consider leaving pets at home or keep them leashed or in the car.

Even the most loveable pet may startle, chase, or harm wildlife—or be injured itself (note bear tracks in sand).

Safety around muskox

Muskox are best enjoyed from a safe distance without unnecessary disturbances. The following pointers will help you avoid unpleasant encounters.

- Muskox may allow you to get surprisingly close. However, they are powerful animals and will react if they feel threatened in their space.

- Pay attention to body language. A muskox that has stopped feeding, walking, or resting has noticed you. It may become agitated and sway its head from side to side. A threatened herd will form a defensive line or circle. Give them room and retreat quickly.

Observe muskox from a safe distance. Retreat if they form a defensive line to reduce disturbance to groups.

- Do not agitate or approach females with their young.

- Bull muskox are more aggressive during the fall breeding season from August through October. Avoid disturbing males in rut.

- Keep dogs under control at all times in muskox country.

- View muskox from at least 150 feet, give groups a wide berth, and don't box them in with people or vehicles.

- If you are charged, run and seek safety. Do not stand your ground.

- Muskox will stand their ground, making it difficult to drive them from an area.

- Feeding muskox is both dangerous and illegal.

No muskox attacks on humans have been reported, but muskox are known to attack and kill dogs. During unexpected close encounters with muskox, try to protect yourself and your dogs.

Safety around moose

Moose are not inherently aggressive. However, a cow protecting her calf or an angry, frightened moose—weighing hundreds of pounds and equipped with a repertoire of powerful kicks and stomps—can be a lethal force. More people are injured by moose than bears in Alaska.

- Give moose plenty of space—at least 100 feet. Make sure both you and the animal have options for a safe, dignified retreat.

- If a moose doesn't yield as you approach, give it the trail.

- Never get between a cow moose and her calf.

- Watch carefully for signs that a moose is upset. Back away slowly and keep your eyes on the animal.

You are probably too close if a moose raises its hackles, pins back its ears, or licks its lips repeatedly. Back away slowly keeping your eye on the animal.

- If you are charged by a moose, run behind a tree or another large object. If you are in the open, run away—moose usually will not chase you very far.

- If a moose knocks you down, curl up in a ball, protect your head with your hands, and hold still until the moose moves a safe distance away.

Safety around bears

Grizzly (brown) bears are found throughout the Seward Peninsula in any habitat type. Bear-human encounters are rare but they do occur, so practice basic bear safety and strive to avoid encounters.

- **Bears don't like surprises.** If you hike away from your car, try to pick an open route. If it's brushy, let bears know of your presence: make noise, sing, talk loudly, or carry a bell. Try to keep the wind at your back so your scent will warn bears of your presence, especially in thick brush. Travel in a group if possible.

- **Pick your path carefully.** Bears, like humans, prefer easy walking and will use a trail, road, river bank, coastline, or lakeshore. Stay alert for tracks in soft ground or sand. Don't set up camp close to natural travel routes. Detour around areas where you see or smell fish or animal carcasses or see scavengers congregating.

Electric fences are easy to install and can protect campsites, fish racks, and cabins from bears. Visit www.alaskabears.alaska.gov to learn more.

- **Don't teach bears that human food or garbage is an easy meal.** Don't bring strong-smelling foods. Cook and store food several hundred yards away from where you will sleep. Keep food and fish smells off your clothing. Keep a clean camp: burn garbage completely and pack out the remains. Burying garbage is a waste of time—bears have great noses and are excellent diggers.

- **Carry bear spray.** Recent studies confirm that bear spray is more effective than firearms in diffusing a close bear encounter. Spray directly at the bear's eyes from very close range—preferably upwind of the bear. Spraying around your camp or on your clothes will not deter a bear and may even attract it.

If a bear cannot tell what you are, it may come closer or stand on its hind legs for a better look or smell.

- **If you do encounter a bear, stay calm— don't run!** You cannot outrun a bear and you may trigger its instinct to chase fleeing animals. Bears sometimes charge within a few feet of a person without making contact. Try to back away slowly and diagonally, but stop and hold your ground if the bear follows.

- **Identify yourself.** Let the bear know you are human. Talk in a normal voice, wave your arms, or join arms with others to try and appear larger. A bear standing on its hind legs is usually curious, not threatening. If the bear comes too close, raise your voice and act more aggressive. Never imitate bear sounds or make a high-pitched squeal.

- **If attacked:** When a grizzly does attack, it is often defending its cubs, its food, or it has been surprised. Lie flat on your stomach or curl into a ball with your hands behind your neck. Typically a bear will break off the attack once it feels it has eliminated the threat. Remain motionless for as long as possible or the bear may renew its attack. In the extremely rare case that a grizzly perceives you as potential food, fight back as hard as you can.

A large male bear displays aggression by popping its jaws, foaming, and stiff-legged strutting.

Seasons of the Seward Peninsula

Many visitors will never experience winter's extremes on the Seward Peninsula, but the seasonal ebb and flow of snow, ice, and permafrost has a profound effect on the environment and the presence of wildlife year-round. Long cold winters and short cool summers typify its subarctic climate while the seasons in-between are more aptly named "break-up" and "freeze-up" than spring and fall. Coastal locations, like Nome, experience some moderating effects from the ocean.

Winter

The winter sun hangs low on the horizon and the snow layer reflects all but a small fraction of solar energy back into the sky. With snowfall averaging about 76 inches a year, the short-legged wooly muskox seeks higher elevations swept clean of snow by winds. Moose hug the river banks where they can browse on tall willows, and foxes travel widely seeking food. At least 29 bird species overwinter here. Gyrfalcons prey on hares and birds. Ptarmigans plunge into snowbanks at night to roost in the snow's warm insulating layer, while redpolls subsist on seeds and nestle in tunnels dug by lemmings. Daylight lasts just under four hours at winter solstice (Dec. 22). Even as the days lengthen, temperatures remain frigid. February is the coldest month when overnight temperatures average about -2°F.

An Arctic fox in its white winter coat rests in a snowdrift.

The showy Kamchatka rhododendron is a welcome sight in spring.

Spring

The sun's rays only begin to warm the land once a critical mass of snow and the ice layer covering the sea and freshwater has melted. This period, called spring break-up, is usually underway by late April. The snow cover melts, the ground thaws, and rivers begin to flow. Meanwhile migrant birds and marine mammals are arriving, heralded by the snow bunting whose rippling whistle can be heard as early as the beginning of March.

Summer

By the time summer bustles in at the end of May, more than 160 species of migratory birds are populating the region, filling the air with their calls, and starting to nest. Many are wetlands birds drawn to lush areas fed by tides and icy meltwater. Wetlands are rich in food sources like aquatic plants and a huge variety of edible invertebrates, including the mosquitoes that bedevil both man and beast when the winds are calm.

Red-necked grebe with chick riding on back.

As summer solstice and its 21 ½ hours of daylight approach, moose on the watch for predators become quite secretive and calve in side-slope willow thickets. By July brown bears frequent streams and rivers to snag salmon headed for spawning grounds. July is also the start of a three-month "wet" season. Though Nome's average 7 ¾ inch annual rainfall is comparable to a desert, this period is characterized by cloudy skies, drizzle and fog, and average temperatures in the high 50's.

Fall

Winter is looming by August and food is growing scarcer making late summer and fall a stressful time for wildlife. Young migratory birds must be strong enough for the long journey south so the adults of some species depart first in order to leave enough food for the offspring. Gray whales head south in August along with many waterfowl and shorebirds. Honking geese and spectacular flights of sandhill cranes, bugling a soft baritone chorus, fill the September skies as they begin their southward migration. Remarkably, a few song bird species (passerines), like the bluethroat, turn westward and depart Alaska for Asia and beyond. Every day the sun dips lower in the sky and the ground loses more heat. By late September, temperatures increasingly linger below freezing. Like spring, fall passes quickly and about a month after freeze-up begins winter has settled back over the land.

Glorious fall colors and termination dust on the mountain tops signal winter is near as great flocks of cranes and geese begin their southward migration.

Wildlife & Subsistence Calendar

Activities (human & wildlife)

Activity	Jan	Feb	Mar	Apr	May	Jun	Jul	Aug	Sep	Oct	Nov	Dec
Catch burbot and pike through holes in river ice	■	■	■	■								
Catch trout through holes in river ice	■	■	■	■						■	■	■
Catch king crabs with crab pots and hand lines through the ice	■	■	■	■								
Pick stinkweed for making medicines	■	■	■	■	■		■	■	■	■	■	■
Hunt muskox (longest season Aug 1 - Mar 15)	■	■	■					■	■	■	■	■
Hunt seals from edge of sea ice or in holes and, by April, in leads	■	■	■	■					■	■		
Hunt caribou	■	■	■							■	■	■
Trap furbearers like fox, wolf, wolverine, mink, beaver, and otter	■	■	■	■								■
Hunt ptarmigan	■	■	■					■	■	■	■	■
Hunt walrus riding on floating ice offshore			■	■	■							
Jig for tomcod through holes in sea ice			■	■							■	■
Golden eagles arrive and occupy nesting locations			■	■								
Large flocks of ptarmigan gather in willows, still mostly white			■	■								
Common ravens begin nesting			■	■	■							
Caribou begin spring migration north to calving grounds				■								
Gulls begin arriving (early April)				■								
Hunt beluga whales in open leads and from ice edge (late April)				■	■							
Hunt early arriving sea ducks and seabirds (late April)				■								
Trap ground squirrels for fur used as fancy parka trim				■					■			
Herd reindeer closer to town for fawning				■								
Brown bears (grizzlies) emerge from hibernation				■								
Baby seals are born				■								
Redpolls and northern shrike begin nesting				■	■							
Reindeer fawning draws predators				■	■							
Muskox calving				■	■	■						
Gather tubers from Eskimo potato plant						■	■			■	■	
Cut seal meat and hang to dry					■							
Hunt bowhead whale (residents of island villages and Wales)					■							
Hunt muskrat and beaver					■							
Hunt ducks, geese, and cranes					■			■	■			
Ptarmigan nesting					■	■						
Sandhill cranes and geese pass overhead on northward migration, some begin to stay by mid-May.					■							
Waterfowl, shorebirds, and numerous migrating birds start arriving by mid-May as snow cover diminishes and ponds thaw.					■							
Wilson's snipe begins calling and aerial displays					■							

Activities (human & wildlife)

Activities (human & wildlife)	Jan	Feb	Mar	Apr	May	Jun	Jul	Aug	Sep	Oct	Nov	Dec
Short-eared owls arrive mid-May and nest in lowland tundra meadows if voles and lemmings are abundant					■							
Pregnant cow moose chase away last year's calves before calving					■							
Gather newly opened willow leaves for eating					■							
Fish for Dolly Varden with rod and reel					■	■		■	■			
Ponds, lakes, and Safety Sound mostly ice-free by late May					■							
Moose calving coincides with leaf-out					■	■						
Most birds are nest building and laying eggs by late May					■	■						
Catch herring at sea with gill net or seine net					■	■						
Catch capelin by dipping net or trash can or hand-picking off sand					■	■						
Gather beach greens and fireweed shoots						■						
Gather seabird and waterfowl eggs						■						
Birds hatching						■	■					
Chum and Chinook salmon begin spawning							■					
Net, cut, dry, smoke, can, and freeze salmon							■	■	■	■		
Gather sourdock, also called wild spinach							■					
Pick and freeze salmonberries							■	■				
Chum and pink salmon spawning until mid-August							■	■				
Fish for coho salmon								■	■	■		
Coho salmon spawning								■	■	■	■	
Pick and freeze blueberries and crowberries								■	■			
Whimbrels and shorebirds begin flocking before migrating								■	■			
Waterfowl begin pre-migration staging									■			
Pick and freeze cranberries									■			
Fish for grayling and whitefish									■	■		
Hunt moose									■			
Harvest reindeer									■			
Sandhill cranes and Canada geese migrating south									■			
Moose are in rut									■	■		
Seine net for whitefish in rivers									■	■		
Snare snowshoe and Alaska hares										■		
Hunt seals in open water										■	■	
Caribou, arrival of migrating animals from north										■		
Short-eared owl, fall migration departure										■		
Dip rainbow smelt from thin lagoon ice w/chicken wire dippers										■		
Jig for tomcod through lagoon and harbor ice										■	■	■
Snowy owl, arrival in some years											■	■
Hunt polar bears in northern regions												■

WILDLIFE HABITATS

In much of the United States, the expanding human population has pushed wildlife onto small islands of natural habitat that can be pinpointed on a map. The reverse is true on the Seward Peninsula. Here humans live on small islands of development surrounded by vast expanses where animals roam wild. This makes it far more difficult to identify specific locations to reliably see wildlife.

This section describes ten basic habitat types that are common along Nome's three major roads and the mammals, birds, and fish that generally live there. Use this information to identify the habitat for a good idea of what animals you may find there.

Coastal Waters and Beaches

Driftwood and logs from far-away forests are deposited on Nome shores by storm-driven wind and waves.

The marine world meets land in this habitat dominated by the action of the wind and sea. Surf-pounded headlands interrupt long sand beaches. In other places, the tundra rolls gently to the coast or waves carve perpetually eroding bluffs, sometimes revealing ancient remains. Salt-tolerant plants thrive among forests of driftwood, and birds and animals ride on wind-driven waves.

Mammals

The scent of dead marine mammals stranded on sandy beaches draws grizzlies from great distances. Both red foxes and Arctic foxes are known to join the beachside banquet. On calm days it is possible to see marine mammals from shore. Look for the "blow" of gray whales as they migrate to summer feeding grounds in the Bering and Chukchi Seas in April and May and return south in October and November. Bowhead

Herds of open range reindeer may seek refuge from mosquitoes by heading to the cooler, breezier coast.

and minke whales migrating many miles offshore aren't usually seen, but large groups of beluga whales often swim near shore in late fall. Killer whales are also present and viewed with overwhelming respect by coastal Natives, as they are never hunted. Neither are the very small harbor porpoises that quietly break the surface, often passing unseen and unheard.

Beluga whales

In open water, the head of a seal may appear briefly then slip below the surface before it can be identified. Occasionally, seals or their pups rest alone on the beach and should not be disturbed. When broken sea ice or shore-fast ice is present, it may afford the occasional glimpse of a hauled-out spotted seal, ringed seal, or bearded seal. Ribbon seals are far less common. Native hunters in small boats pursue walruses, but the animals are not viewable from shore. Polar bears, common further north, rarely venture down to the southern portion of the Seward Peninsula.

Birds

The light gray Arctic tern flies nearly 10,000 miles from its wintering grounds in Antarctica to breed and raise young in nests that are often no more than a slight indentation on sandy beaches. Common eiders use a protected upper vegetated beach to nest and are often seen in marine waters. Black-legged kittiwakes, common murres, thick-billed murres, tufted puffins, horned puffins, and pelagic cormorants, which

Arctic tern

otherwise spend their lives at sea, nest on coastal bluffs and can be seen feeding or flying along the coastline. Loons fly between inland nesting sites and fishing grounds in marine waters. Shorebirds, gulls, and waterfowl rest and feed on beaches and tidal flats, especially as they prepare for their fall migration south. Savannah sparrows and Lapland longspurs are abundant in the tall grasses that border the road along Safety Sound.

Fish and other marine creatures

Shortly after spring break-up, young salmon and Dolly Varden fingerlings leave the rivers for marine waters where they provide food for predatory fish and birds. At the same time, capelin (also called candlefish or cigarfish) often come to the beach in the evening to spawn—and are harvested by people or snatched up by Arctic terns. Herring, which move along the coast in springtime, are also harvested but are too big for the terns. In early July, adult salmon begin returning to their rivers of origin to spawn. Occasionally, they are seen schooling at river mouths or jumping near shore.

Dolly Varden fingerling

As the ice begins to form on the coastal lagoons in fall, schools of tomcod (saffron cod) can be seen just off the beach or in lagoon entrances. They are often accompanied by rainbow smelt and followed by bobbing seals or groups of gulls circling in a clustered feeding melee. Fall storms often make for interesting finds on the beach, turning up cockles, soft shell clams, razor clams, sea urchins, starfish, sand dollars, jellyfish, whelks, moon snails, sea strawberries, and blue mussels near rocky headlands.

Catching king crab through holes in the spring shore-fast ice is a popular local subsistence activity. Starfish, slimy sculpin, sea urchins, soft-bellied crabs, and helmet crabs sometimes appear in people's crab pots as well.

Harvesting king crabs in winter.

Estuaries and Lagoons

Protected lagoon waters offer birds and fish a place to feed, rest, and raise their young.

Tides and storms periodically force salt water inland while clear-flowing rivers steadily deliver inland waters to the sea. In this brackish mixing zone, fish and wildlife adapt or shift with the fluctuating border between fresh and salt water. Rivers often snake through coastal lowlands and around sand spits to enter the sea, but in some cases a barrier beach, ringed with salt-tolerant plants and grasses, separates fresh water from the sea. The resulting lagoon offers a sheltered feeding, resting, and nursery zone to birds and fish alike.

Mammals

Arctic ground squirrels den in the soft sandy soils, with a large piece of driftwood hiding the entrance to their burrows. The squirrels may drown in unusually high fall storm surges, and grizzlies easily dig for them in the loose soil. Red foxes—and the occasional Arctic fox—may pass through the tall grasses hunting for the eggs or chicks of nesting waterfowl, and Alaska hares are often present in fall.

Several species of fish enter lagoons at freeze-up as a way of escaping predatory seals. Seals cannot breathe under the solid layer of ice but will congregate at a lagoon's open water entrance to feed on fish as they enter.

Red fox kits linger in tall grasses near their den.

Birds

This habitat is used primarily by loons, waterfowl, shorebirds, terns, and gulls that feed on abundant juvenile fish. Lagoons are especially important in spring when meltwater appears at the mouths of rivers and the near shoreline edges of lagoons. This early open water attracts large flocks of birds returning to the area. Both glaucous gulls and black brant may nest in the salt grass meadows, and common eiders often nest in colonies on islands within protected lagoon waters.

Shorebirds gather along the edges of the lagoon and on muddy tidal islands during the spring and early summer. Large numbers of tundra swans and sandhill cranes arrive at Safety Sound in the spring and remain throughout the summer. During fall, huge flocks of waterfowl and shorebirds gather at Safety Sound prior to migrating south.

Tundra swans and their young, called cygnets, leave the nest after hatching and forage in lush vegetation adjacent to lagoons.

Fish

Three types of flatfish—starry flounder, Alaska plaice, and yellowfin sole—live in lagoons and often move up into the freshwater streams that feed the lagoons. In summer the lagoons serve as a critical nursery for juvenile Arctic char and chum, silver, and red salmon, which in turn feed the many birds that congregate here. At freeze-up tomcod, rainbow smelt, and several species of sculpin enter the lagoons seeking protection from the seals. This is a popular time for locals to chip holes through the ice and jig for tomcods. Blackfish and stickleback live in lagoons without an outlet, feeding on insect larvae.

Rainbow smelt

River Valleys

River valleys offer shelter and nourishment to an enormous diversity of wildlife throughout the year.

Clear, fast-flowing waters edged with gravel bars, riverbanks lush with willows and wildflowers, slow-moving sloughs and seasonal ponds, and a vegetated floodplain offer something for almost every wild animal at one time of the year or another. Riverbanks receive a good supply of fresh water and nutrients, which produce abundant and diverse vegetation such as shrubs, willows, grasses and sedges. Generally permafrost-free, they also allow for greater root development and tree-like growth and—in some areas—cottonwood or spruce trees.

Mammals

In late May and early June, cow moose use the dense vegetation in river bottoms to protect newborn calves from predators, like grizzlies. Moose and reindeer feed voraciously on young, protein-packed willow leaves, which support the rapid growth of their antlers. On hot summer days, muskox may seek shade among the taller riverbank shrubs and cool themselves in the water. Grizzlies drawn to rivers to feed on spawning salmon are joined by hungry foxes and wolves. While moose often disperse up smaller tributaries and hillside stands of willows in summer, they typically return to the river valleys in winter where the tall willows remaining above the snowdrifts offer critical food and shelter.

Bull moose

Beavers are year-round residents that build dams and lodges in side channels and slower moving waters. Muskrats and their "push-ups"—small, cave-like structures where they can rest and sometimes eat—are abundant some years and scarce in others. If river otters are present, you may see them sliding on banks, swimming, or eating freshly caught fish and invertebrates along the riverbank.

Mink feed on voles, shrews, small birds, bird eggs, insects, and fish. Red foxes prey on numerous small birds and mammals drawn to the rivers. Porcupines feed on willow bark along river bottoms.

Birds

Small groups of harlequin ducks and red-breasted mergansers often cruise the river's faster currents. In contrast, large groups of mew gulls and glaucous gulls prefer the slower moving water and large gravel bars. Arctic terns hover and dive for small fish. Small-bodied shorebirds

Harlequin ducks breed in cold, fast-flowing streams and locate their nests on the ground near the water.

use gravel bars and islands for nesting and feeding. In late summer and fall gulls, ravens, and the occasional sandhill crane feed on the carcasses of spawned-out salmon. The dark-gray, robin-sized American dipper is a year-round resident that nests on moist mossy cliffs or under bridges and may be seen bobbing or "dipping" at the water's edge. Cliff swallows often construct gourd-shaped mud nests under bridges and can be seen at river crossings swooping after insects. Bank swallows excavate nesting burrows in cut-banks above the river's high-water zone where silt layers provide locations for burrow-sites that are used from year to year.

The mix of tall and medium height willows are home to myriad songbirds. Common and hoary redpolls are present, as are fox, golden-crowned, white-crowned, and American tree sparrows. Look also for the eye-catching yellow warbler and the much sought after bluethroat. In spring male willow ptarmigan with their dark-brown heads and necks perch in the upper branches of willows to feed on protein-rich buds and gain strength for their courtship activities. In winter large flocks of willow ptarmigan feed in the dense willow thickets and burrow into loose snow at night to roost.

Fish

On the Seward Peninsula you may see coho, sockeye, chum, pink, and Chinook salmon returning to rivers to spawn. Also present are resident species: Arctic gray-ling, Dolly Varden, burbot (freshwater ling-cod), northern pike, and several species of whitefish. If you look closely, you may find sculpins, sticklebacks, and blackfish in

A chum salmon spawning.

ponds, side channels, and sloughs that are connected to the river system. These floodplain ponds also provide rearing habitat for juvenile Arctic grayling, Dolly Varden, and silver salmon.

Wet Tundra and Ponds

Tundra ponds produce swarms of mosquitoes that become a summer banquet drawing millions of birds north each spring.

This tundra calls for tall rubber boots and insect repellant! While not the favored habitat of humans, it is home to a multitude of small rodents that are food for larger animals. Ponds, marshes, and sloughs are critical breeding grounds for a multitude of waterfowl and the insects they feed upon. The swarms of summer mosquitoes provide a tundra banquet that draws millions of birds north each spring.

Mammals

Lemmings, voles, and shrews find abundant food and nesting sites in this lowland habitat. They reproduce rapidly for several years until they have consumed all the available food, which leads to their dispersal or a population crash. They are preyed upon by wolves, red foxes, weasels, and mink, which also hunt birds and steal eggs from the nests tucked into sedges and

Beaver eat bark, roots, grasses, and aquatic plants of all kinds.

grasses. Muskrats inhabit area ponds and so do beaver, which build dams and large, easy-to-spot lodges from nearby stands of willow and cottonwood. Moose sometimes stand knee-deep in ponds feeding on aquatic vegetation with their heads fully submerged. In summer, muskox and reindeer are drawn to sourdock, cloud berries (salmon berries), and other wetland plants.

Birds

Ponds and small lakes are popular nesting areas for red-throated loons. Delicate red-necked phalaropes are often seen at pond edges dabbing at food churned to the surface by their spinning in place. Common waterfowl that nest on or near ponds and small lakes include Canada goose, northern pintail, green-wing teal, tundra swan, and American wigeon. The small, white mew gull (with black wingtips) nests

Delicate red-necked phalaropes are often seen at pond edges dabbing at food churned to the surface by their spinning.

in similar areas, as does the Wilson's snipe. The familiar "winnowing" sound of the male snipe is made by air passing through its outer tail feathers as it dives during aerial courtship flights high above the ground. Sandhill cranes nest here. In the fall large flocks may be seen circling overhead or resting in wetlands on their migration south. While savannah sparrow and Lapland longspur populate the open meadows, white-crowned and American tree sparrows frequent the shrubby edges of ponds.

Fish

Ponds stained brown by tannins generally have little fresh water inflow and no fish. Clear spring-fed ponds are more likely to have fish. Some tundra ponds are shallow and freeze to the bottom, eliminating the possibility of fish. Deeper ponds that don't freeze completely may have blackfish, sculpins, and stickle-

backs. The presence of the tall felt-leaf willow often indicates unfrozen soils and a pond deep enough to provide the nutrients, oxygen, and year-round water fish need to survive.

A river otter dined on three-spined sticklebacks and later eliminated their prickly spines, as evidenced by this otter scat.

Tundra Meadows

The abundance of clumps of sedges or grasses (called tussocks) makes walking difficult in this habitat.

This broad, rolling habitat of meadows interspersed with low shrubs is widespread on much of the Seward Peninsula and the abundance of clumps of sedges or grasses (called tussocks) can make walking difficult. The berry picking is good, however, because this tundra is a little higher and drier than wet tundra. Seasonal frost action can shape this land into small grassy mounds (called hummocks), circular peat rings, and sometimes multi-sided polygons that can be seen from a high vantage point. Less common are pingos: small, domed hills with an ice core and a covering of soil and vegetation, which occasionally rise above the surrounding flat tundra landscape.

Mammals

It is not unusual to see locally-owned herds of free-ranging—meaning no fences keep them in a particular area—reindeer grazing in tundra meadows. Caribou are occasionally sighted in the more northern reaches of the Seward Peninsula. Grizzlies, foxes, wolves, moose, and on rare occasions, a solitary

Reindeer grazing in tundra meadows.

wolverine also travel across this rolling terrain in search of food, shelter, or mating opportunities. During summer months muskox fatten up on the abundant sedges, grasses, and berries before the plants are buried in snow. In terms of sheer abundance, shrews, voles, and lemmings far outnumber larger mammals and are food sources for wolves and foxes. In the Arctic many plant seeds are dispersed by lemmings, voles, ground squirrels, and a multitude of seed-eating birds. Some animals prefer dry seeds, others prefer berries. Five varieties of berries grow in the Arctic: blueberries, cranberries, cloudberries, bearberries, and crowberries.

This red-backed vole resembles a lemming but is smaller and has a longer tail.

Birds

Long-tailed jaegers hover in the wind balancing with their long, slender tails as they hunt for small mammals, bird eggs, or newly hatched chicks of tundra-nesting birds. Short-eared owls also hunt this rodent-rich habitat, as may the occasional snowy owl when voles and lemmings are abundant. The rodent-hunting rough-legged hawk soars high in its search for food, while northern harriers glide low over the tundra looking for small rodents and birds—especially where the habitat borders wetlands.

The brightly-colored yellow wagtail "wags" its long tail up and down when perched on a tundra mound. This relatively small bird makes a yearly migratory flight to Australia for the winter. Two similar-looking large-bodied shorebirds that nest atop the grassy hummocks are the whimbrel with its long, downward-curved bill and the bar-tailed godwit with its slightly turned-up bill. Bar-tailed godwits fly nonstop from Southwestern Alaska to their wintering grounds in New Zealand and Australia.

A whimbrel nesting among tundra wildflowers.

Side Slopes: Medium Shrubs

Moisture-laden soils over permafrost slowly creep downward in a process called solifluction.

Between the wetter lowlands and the high and dry rocky hilltops, bands of willows, alders, and taller vegetation traverse drier slopes of tundra meadow. Like warm icing sliding down the side of a cake, moisture-laden soil lying over permanently frozen ground creeps downhill in slow-moving waves—a process called solifluction. The moist leading edge promotes the growth of flowering plants and shrubs that are taller than the surrounding drier soils can support. The alternating bands of vegetation offer wildlife of all sizes an attractive combination of food and shelter.

Mammals

Grizzlies typically den on south-facing slopes where they graze on the first succulent green sprouts in spring. Throughout the summer they roam the hillsides digging for roots and arctic ground squirrels and feeding on a variety of grasses, sedges, horsetails, flowering plants, and berries. Moose typically

A grizzly sow and cubs crossing a side slope.

winter in the tall willows of the lower river valleys but move to the willowed side slopes and tributaries in spring and stay throughout the summer and fall. Groups of muskox often feed along the side slopes, leaving wisps and wads of their soft underfur—called **qiviut**—hanging in the willow branches. Occasionally, during the first warm days of spring, they will comb out larger clumps of shedding fur by pushing through dense willow thickets. At any time of year, wolves or wolverines may traverse these slopes although sightings are uncommon. When vole populations are high, hillsides may be riddled with small burrow entrances that lead to

an extensive network of tunnels under winter's snows. These tunnels attract, and sometimes house, least weasels that prey on the voles. Snowshoe hares may be found on the side slopes of Golden Gate, Cape Nome, and the Council area.

When running in snow, the least weasel places its hind feet in its front feet tracks. As a result, the trail looks like a line of twin prints.

Birds

Where roads traverse this habitat, you may see willow ptarmigan and broods of chicks filling their crops with fine roadside gravels to aid their digestion. The small and somewhat drab Arctic warbler nests here, gorging itself on insects to fuel its winter migration to the Philippines. Another small bird from across the Bering Strait is the ground-nesting and appropriately-named bluethroat. The gray-cheeked thrush builds its nest in willow shrubs, as does the female common redpoll, which sometimes reuses a nest from the previous year. The male fox sparrow sings from the tips of tall shrubs while the female builds the nest. Rough-legged hawks soar overhead searching for small mammals and birds, while golden eagles hunt for ground squirrels, ptarmigan, or other larger prey. Gyrfalcons use power-ful dives or direct rapid flight—sometimes very close to the ground—to make surprise attacks on unsuspecting ground squirrels, ptarmigan, and other large birds.

A willow ptarmigan (male in spring) taking a dust bath sends gravel flying.

Dwarf Tundra: Ridgelines & Hilltops

Permafrost and high winds on hilltops make it difficult for all but the hardiest plants to thrive.

In this high, dry, windblown region of ridgetops and high domes, the plants are small and unique and the wildlife is hardy. Some sites are covered by a low, thin mat of soil and vegetation, while other areas may be mostly rocks or gravel with isolated clusters of plants. Without taller vegetation to trap blowing snow, these areas often blow clear in winter, offering easier winter footing and exposed vegetation for grazing animals. In spring the cleared areas provide snow-free nesting locations for early-breeding shorebirds. Dwarf tundra is also found in certain lowland areas like the road to Woolley Lagoon.

Mammals

This is the domain of muskox, especially in winter when these short-legged relatives of wild goats gather to avoid deep or drifted snow. Caribou may also travel the windswept ridges in winter where they can feed on lichens and sedges without having to use energy to break and paw through the snow— a process called cratering. In spring grizzlies often dig up large areas of hillside to

Muskox find food and refuge from deep snows on these wind-swept dwarf tundra hilltops.

feed on roots and Arctic ground squirrels. Reindeer in summer may seek the high ridges or cluster on small snow patches to try and escape the relentless swarms of flies and mosquitoes. Wolves and the elusive wolverine may traverse this habitat at any time of year as they move from one drainage system to the next in their unending search for food.

Birds

Dwarf tundra hilltops provide nesting sites for Lapland longspurs, horned larks, American pipits, and American golden-plovers. In breeding season, the male Lapland longspur rises from the ground in an aerial display then glides down on outstretched wings and spreading tail—singing out as it approaches the ground. Where a rocky field meets dwarf tundra, look for the flash of the bold white-and-black tail of a northern wheatear.

*The shrill **ku-wheep** of the American golden-plover can be heard as they skitter from point to point, displaying their black undersides.*

Vegetation may be sparse, but birds still find plenty to feed on. Hilltops harbor tiny flowers that are often miniature versions of plants found in warmer climes. Though small, these flowers are a bountiful source of nectar for the insects that rely on them, insects that are in turn an important food source for many birds.

Clockwise from top right: Arctic forget-me-not, glacier avens, mountain harebell, mountain avens, alpine azalea.

Rocky Outcrops and Inland Cliffs

Predators use these vantage points to scan the surrounding landscape for prey.

Exposed vertical cliffs of bedrock, rocky outcrops and slopes, and granite tors make up this habitat. There is little soil to nourish plants, but raptors (birds of prey) use the outcrops as vantage points to search for prey and leave behind remains of uneaten prey, feces, and castings (regurgitated pellets of undigested fur, feathers, teeth, and bones of eaten prey). Red foxes also use these vantage points and leave behind droppings or scat, sometimes with undigested plant seeds in them. Where these natural waste products leach nutrients into the rocky terrain, they fertilize an otherwise inhospitable spot and create a tiny oasis of diverse and unexpected plants.

Mammals

Few mammals other than Arctic ground squirrels regularly reside in this environment though red foxes, wolves, and wolverine will use these high vantage points to scan the landscape for prey,

A gray wolf lopes along a ridge, silhouetted against a dusky sky.

much as Native hunters have done for thousands of years. Muskox inhabiting the surrounding uplands may use the rocks as defensive positions or scratching posts, leaving tufts of underwool clinging to the rock. Grizzlies may establish regular routes through certain rock outcrops and leave lasting impressions in softer soils by repeatedly placing their feet in the same tracks year after year.

Birds

Cliff faces are the haunts of raptors and ravens where each builds a different style of stick-nest. The common raven nest is small and loose, built with bulky sticks and often found under a rocky overhang. Rough-legged hawks weave a nest of small, fine-diameter sticks in more exposed areas. Golden eagles build impressively large nests of medium-sized sticks that they add to year after year, forming a huge column of material. Gyrfalcons and peregrine falcons don't build their own nests, preferring to occupy a previously built stick-nest or use an open rock terrace or ledge to raise their young. For all species, alternate nest sites accumulate through time so pairs are able to find a suitable site under varying spring weather conditions. Canada geese have been known to use stick-nests on riverside cliffs built by one of the raptor species. When scanning for a raptor nest or perching site, look for rocks that appear stained, painted, or encrusted with a bright orange to rust-red color.

Rough-legged hawk chicks in a nest decorated with lemming carcasses.

In summer raptors prey upon small mammals and the numerous species of birds that migrate to the area, while winter food is limited to the few resident prey species. Golden eagles hunt primarily for ground squirrels, Alaska hares, and ptarmigan. Gyrfalcons rely on ptarmigan and hares in winter and ground squirrels, jaegers, gulls, waterfowl, and Alaska hares in summer. Rough-legged hawks use their talons to capture small mammals and birds. Peregrine falcons feed almost exclusively on small to medium-sized birds including shorebirds, seabirds, terns, and songbirds. Other species often seen in this habitat include Say's phoebe and cliff swallow. The small, white snow bunting nests in crevices among the boulders close to low-growing tundra.

Rust-colored patches, common on the rock faces around a sticknest, are a type of lichen that grows naturally in these highly fertilized locations. Often you will also see streamers of whitewash from the chalky portion of fecal material.

Boreal Forest

Black spruce and white spruce are the most common conifers in the boreal forest. Their relatively shallow roots can take hold in a thin layer of unfrozen soil.

The only extensively forested area within the road system lies at the end of Council Road. Dominated by conifer and deciduous tree species, this habitat mostly follows well-drained river bottoms and side slopes. It is the westernmost extent of interior Alaska's boreal forest and home to wildlife that is typical of the northern forests.

The dominant plants are black and white spruce mixed with large stands of cottonwood (balsam poplar) and tall or medium thickets of willow, alder, and dwarf birch. Black spruce can grow in the cooler, wetter soils that are underlain with permafrost but are generally smaller than white spruce. White spruce requires elevated, warmer south-facing slopes or the thawed ground along riverbanks. Cottonwood, paper birch, and the tallest shrubs also require thawed ground to thrive. Much of the boreal forest in the Council area is semi-open. The understory is interspersed with highbush cranberry and wild rose with a ground cover of lichens and mosses.

Mammals

The spruce forest is home to marten, a member of the weasel family that seeks shelter and protection in spruce trees and depends on fallen logs and debris for denning. They typically hunt for voles, lemmings, and shrews where the forest edge meets bogs and wetlands. Red squirrels are common boreal forest residents often seen cutting and storing a winter stash of green spruce cones—one of their primary foods. Lynx generally thrive in this area in

Marten primarily eat voles but also carrion, birds and squirrels. They can even be cannibalistic when food is scarce.

Porcupines are often found in spruce forests and are one of the few species that eats the bark of living spruce trees.

years when their primary prey—the snowshoe hare—is abundant. Hares feed primarily on willows and dwarf birch, their population increasing over a period of years until they have depleted the available food. Willows and dwarf birch also protect themselves from being overbrowsed by developing a toxin distasteful to hares. The hare population crashes, browsing ends, the willows recover, and the cycle begins anew.

Beavers are common along the major rivers and many smaller tributaries and creeks. Porcupines are often found in spruce forests where they feed on the bark of spruce trees. Moose inhabit forested areas wherever willows are found but tend to occupy higher wooded draws in summer before moving down to the river bottoms in winter. The boreal forest is among the many habitats used by grizzlies, wolverines, and wolves.

Birds

Birds common to Interior Alaska's boreal forest are also found in the fringes of spruce forest that extend onto the Seward Peninsula. Gray jays nest fairly high up in spruce trees around Council. The heavy-billed, seed-eating pine grosbeak is present, as is the more delicate, insect-eating ruby-crowned kinglet. Black-capped chickadees are widespread throughout the boreal forest region. The less common boreal chickadee nests in the Council area in the cavities of spruce trees. Belted kingfishers nest in mud burrows along waterways. The osprey, a fish-eating raptor, nests along the Niukluk River where it hovers above the water and plunges, grasping the fish in its talons. The solitary sandpiper, a woodland shorebird species, migrates to this area

A gray jay, true to its nicknames "meat bird" and "camp robber," plucks fat from a hunter's moose carcass.

from Central and South America. Other songbirds associated with this area's forest habitat include varied thrush, blackpoll warbler, and yellow-rumped warbler.

Fish

All five species of salmon (chum, pink, coho, sockeye, and Chinook) are present in the Niukluk River, as are Arctic grayling, northern pike, Arctic lampreys, and sculpin. Also present are small crustaceans called isopods (or toe-biters).

Human-modified

Lines etched in the rock face are sections of man-made ditches that once served the area's gold mining operations. Dense zones of vegetation that grow along the ditches are used by some animals for shelter.

Humans need the same things as wildlife to survive—shelter, food, water, and space. To meet our habitat needs, especially this far north, we must modify the environment around us. Historic-use sites, contemporary homebuilding, road construction, and community and industrial development all bring changes to the natural landscape. In securing our own habitat needs, we alter the habitat negatively for some species while creating new opportunities for others.

Mammals

In the early part of the 20th century, mining activities were widespread across much of the Seward Peninsula. Miners dug hundreds of miles of ditch lines across slopes to deliver water needed for removing the overburden and sluicing the diggings. These ditches introduced a line of added moisture across drier slopes, which encouraged the growth of willows, alders, and cottonwoods. This dense zone of vegetation is a

An Arctic ground squirrel is at home amid the rubble of a derelict structure.

good place to check for wildlife. It's used by prey species for forage, bedding, and protection while also drawing in predators searching for prey.

Landfills and dumps naturally draw foxes—and even grizzlies and wolves—with the smell of discarded food. The sound of water running through culverts attracts beavers and triggers their instinct to construct dams. Moose appear to have learned that their predators, grizzlies and wolves, tend to avoid areas where people live. Ermine (also called short-tailed weasels) seek out caches of meat or dog food and find an abundance of hiding and denning sites in outbuildings and under lumber piles and old boats. Arctic ground squirrels frequent most area roadways because the loosened soils along road shoulders make for easy burrow construction. Grizzlies are attracted to camps, fish or meat racks, and improperly disposed garbage.

Birds

Elevated roadbeds and roadway cuts through hills catch snow and channel summer rains. The willows, shrubs, and taller wildflowers that grow in these pockets of higher moisture attract songbirds, which in turn draw raptors that feed on the small birds. Dumps and landfills are also magnets for scavenging gulls and ravens. Ptarmigan are drawn to freshly plowed roads in winter looking for gravel to aid digestion. Causeways, piers, and jetties attract harlequin ducks. These structures also serve as resting and gathering spots for other sea-going ducks and birds. Old dredge ponds and even roadside ponds can attract waterfowl, phalaropes, loons, and terns.

Common ravens take advantage of human construction, building their conspicuous stick nests on old dredges, shipping containers at the port, cabins, and these Anvil Mountain antenna supports.

Cliff swallows often build their gourd-shaped mud nests under bridges.

Common redpolls, American robins, tree swallows, snow and McKay's buntings, and a few white wagtails have all made themselves at home in human neighborhoods. Common ravens often stash food in nooks and crannies of roofs and other elevated sites where they roost. During lean times, they will investigate potential food caches by poking and peering. Cliff swallows also make good use of bridges for nest building. Say's phoebes occasionally choose remote, largely undisturbed cabins and old dredges as nest sites.

Fish

Mineral sediment stirred up by mining, road construction, and even personal vehicles driven across rivers can coat salmon spawning gravels. This process—called concretion—prevents oxygen and nutrients from circulating to the eggs and eliminates the flushing away of waste products. The eggs cannot survive, resulting in fish runs that are reduced or eliminated.

In the case of hard rock mining, the blasting and crushing of rock that contains naturally occurring heavy metals may expose these contaminants to weathering at unnaturally high rates. When these contaminants enter streams, they can kill aquatic life. Offshore dredging on a large scale can also impact the habitat of marine life.

Culverts, when properly sized and placed, have been successfully used to allow fish movement under roadbeds. A hanging culvert—one that creates a waterfall on the downstream side instead of being level with the waterway—can present a barrier to migrating salmon during low water periods. Today's road construction techniques incorporate appropriate culverts and the construction of roadside pools and riffles in an effort to preserve salmon spawning habitat. Placer mines use settling ponds to remove sediments before water is returned to the natural system.

Dredging riverbeds can eliminate the pools and riffles that salmon, like these pinks, need to spawn.

WILDLIFE FACTS

Land Mammals

Moose

The largest members of the deer family (cervid), moose are relative newcomers to the Seward Peninsula. They began arriving in the 1930s from Interior Alaska, following a natural range expansion possibly related to climate warming. They found suitable habitat in the region thanks to the effects of mining on the land, which encouraged the dense growth of their preferred food: the willow.

A calf will grow to more than 10 times its birth mass in its first five months.

Spring calving season

As the snow melts in spring, moose begin to leave their wintering grounds along river bottoms and disperse into willowed tributaries, side drainages, and slopes. Pregnant cows aggressively chase away their confused yearling calves before giving birth around the last week of May or first week of June—about the time the willows leaf out. This provides some cover for the newborn calves, which are vulnerable to grizzly bear predation. Cow moose with young calves move around very little and are very protective. They become less secretive as the calves grow older and may leave their young resting in the bushes while they feed. Twin calves are often observed in early June but, due to predators, rarely do both survive.

Seeking summer food

By summer most moose, except for some cows with young calves, have shifted their range onto side slopes and upper tributaries. This ensures that enough of the taller willows, which grow along river bottoms, are preserved for food and shelter in winter when other shorter willows are buried deep in snow.

Fall excitement

The breeding season, or rut, typically runs from mid-September to mid-October and peaks the first week of October. Cow moose tend to group together during this time, usually in the headwaters of drainages on willowed slopes. A single mature bull does most breeding but younger bulls may linger close by hoping for a chance. Bulls may spar but the jousting—while dramatic—usually results in serious wounds only when the bulls are equal in size, strength, and determination.

Winter in the willows

As snow accumulates, moose tend to move back to river bottoms seeking the taller felt-leaf willows that typically grow along the banks where the ground is free of permafrost. Moose are weakest and most vulnerable in late winter.

Management

When setting hunting seasons and harvest quotas, ADF&G biologists in Nome generally strive for a sizable harvest while leaving enough bulls to breed all the cows during the early part of the rut.

Bulls grow antlers each summer and shed them in winter, usually around December and January.

They also try to ensure that the moose population doesn't grow so large that their food supply is depleted. Overbrowsing could result in a population crash after just one or two high snowfall winters. Biologists look for signs of stress like "brooming." That's when willow tips that are nipped year after year form a tight bunch of stems like the head of a broom. Biologists also weigh ten-month-old moose calves in areas of concern to determine the nutritional value and health of the habitat. Low calf weights combined with heavily browsed habitat may prompt biologists to open a cow hunt in order to quickly reduce or stabilize population levels and avoid a crash.

Twin yearlings have just been weighed by an ADF&G biologist at about 380 pounds each.

Grizzly bears also put pressure on the moose population by preying on calves. ADF&G has increased the legal bear harvest through longer hunting seasons in an effort to boost the moose population. Balancing hunting pressures, predation, and the availability of winter willows remains the challenge and goal of maintaining healthy moose populations.

Viewing tips

Moose can show up in a number of places—one was even spotted swimming past Nome—but willows are their preferred habitat. You may see just a head and two big ears pop up from the brush. In the fall a flash of light may be the sun reflecting off a bull's antlers. At a good vantage point, use binoculars to scan the appropriate habitat.

Reindeer

Reindeer and caribou belong to the deer family, are members of the same species, and can interbreed. But, unlike their wild cousins, reindeer are semi-domesticated. For centuries, Arctic and subarctic people have herded reindeer, culling animals that display wild or exploratory behavior. This genetic separation has resulted in subtle physical differences between reindeer and caribou. Reindeer have shorter legs, slightly larger

Subtle differences have developed over time between semi-domesticated reindeer (pictured above) and their close relatives, the caribou.

noses, smaller antlers, and occasionally have white spots on their hide (some are even entirely white). They are very herd-oriented, while caribou often scatter across miles of open country. A reindeer may also be sporting an ear tag.

History of Nome reindeer

The first domesticated reindeer were imported to western Alaska from Siberia in the late 19th century arriving aboard the U.S. Revenue Cutter, Bear. The Bear's Capt. Jack Healy and Presbyterian missionary Sheldon Jackson wanted to provide

Sinrock Mary seated in a reindeer corral.

a new livelihood and food source for coastal Natives whose traditional foods like seal, walrus, and whale were being depleted in unregulated commercial harvests. Chukchi herders from the Russian Far East were also brought over to teach the Alaska Inupiat how to raise and herd reindeer. Mary Antisar'look, a local half-Inupiat and half-Russian woman, played a valuable role as translator. She and her Inupiat husband, Charlie, eventually owned a reindeer herd and lived at Sinrock about 40 miles west of present day Nome. Mary kept the herd after her husband's death and made her fortune selling meat during Nome's gold rush. Known as "Sinrock Mary, Queen of the Reindeer," she later relocated to Unalakleet, a village southeast of Nome, where she taught others the art of reindeer herding.

Mary's chief competitors were Minnesota transplants, Carl and Alfred Lomen. During the 1920s, the Lomen brothers built a successful meatpacking industry selling reindeer meat to markets from Brooklyn to San Francisco. It was thanks to their clever ad campaign in 1926 that Santa's reindeer-drawn sleigh became a Christmas tradition. The market for Lomen Company products grew steadily in the Lower 48. In fact the Lomens were so successful at promoting reindeer that the beef lobby worked hard for passage of the Reindeer Act of 1937, which restricted ownership of reindeer in Alaska to Natives only.

In the mid-1990s, 15 well-established reindeer herds were in Native ownership on the Seward Peninsula. The meat was sold in villages and Nome grocery stores, and a large market in Korea for antlers in velvet made the herds quite profitable. In the late 1990s, however, the Western Arctic caribou herd began migrating farther west into the Seward Peninsula in winter. In some years more than 100,000 caribou swarmed across the reindeer ranges and swept the reindeer into their herd as they returned to North Slope calving grounds in spring. By 2006 less than half of the reindeer remained in the western and southern areas of the peninsula. Nevertheless, a strong market continues for reindeer meat and herders are working to rebuild their herds and pass their animals, skills, and knowledge onto a new generation of Native herders.

Management

Reindeer are privately-managed by individuals with family and community support. This includes moving reindeer to new grazing areas, protecting them from predators, and corralling them for counting, shots, tagging, and research. Some herders move their animals closer to human settlements during the fawning season

Reindeer are regularly rounded up in a reindeer corral for tagging, shots, and antler removal.

to better protect them from predation by grizzlies, wolves, and the occasional wolverine or golden eagle.

ADF&G provides reindeer herders with information on caribou herd locations so they can move their animals out of range of migrating caribou. The Western Arctic caribou herd migrates onto the peninsula in the fall and back out in the spring, moving between the Brooks Range and North Slope to the Nulato Hills and Seward Peninsula twice a year. Unlike caribou, reindeer are privately-owned and may not be hunted without prior permission from the herder.

Viewing Tips

Reindeer are often spotted near Nome (especially at fawning time in late April and early May) and grazing near the roadways throughout the summer. Caribou are seldom seen on the road system except at the north end of the Kougarok Road in late fall. Contact the Reindeer Herders Association (443-4378 or 443-4377) in Nome for more information.

Muskox

Muskox, which are related to sheep and goats, are called **itomingmak** in Inupiaq, meaning "the animal with skin like a beard." Alaska's original muskox disappeared in the early 1900s from overhunting and, perhaps, unfavorable climatic conditions, but a reintroduction program has been successful so far. In 1930, 34 muskox from East Greenland were taken to Fairbanks then transplanted to Nunivak Island in the Bering Sea where they multiplied and thrived. In 1970, 36 animals from the island were released near Feather River Bridge on Teller Road. Eleven years later, another 35 were released at the Port Clarence Coast Guard Station, 15 miles west of Teller. As of 2010 the Seward Peninsula population was an estimated 2,616 muskox, a slight decline from 2007.

Defense, group structure and movements

When disturbed, a herd of muskox typically forms a tight defensive circle to successfully repel bear and wolf attacks. However, if the herd panics and runs, a predator can easily take an animal from behind. Bears are becoming increasing adept at preying on muskox in this manner.

Muskox are gregarious and a winter herd may include up to 75 animals of bulls, cows, and young of all ages.

Muskox often group in large herds of bulls, cows, and young of all ages but lone bulls or bachelor herds of two to 15 bulls also roam widely in winter, seeking suitable food and habitat. As the snow melts in spring, large herds usually break into smaller groups that disperse throughout the area. They maintain consistent summer and winter ranges although predation, hunting pressure, scarcity of food, and other factors may cause them to relocate, sometimes a long distance away.

Savoring spring and summer

As the snow melts on the southern slopes, the herds move down the mountainside to feed on vegetation and emerging shoots in the tundra meadows. The new calves are playful and kick up their heels as the adults graze. This is a good time for local residents to go qiviut picking: collecting the wisps and wads of the soft muskox undercoat that catch on willow branches.

Muskox shed a downy underwool, which is spun into yarn and used by knitters to make warm scarves and hats.

In early summer muskox feed heavily on new greens that appear along the lower slopes. On warm days the entire herd may sprawl in still lingering snowfields or disappear into the riverside willows to feed on lush grasses, escape the summer heat, and enjoy a playful romp in the water. Later in summer they are often seen in high meadows resting or grazing on grasses, sedges, horsetails, flowering plants, and berries as they store fat reserves for the long winter.

Fall rut and winter survival

The rut can be dramatic during muskox breeding season from late July through September. Dominant bulls form harems of up to 15 cows and juveniles, and they fend off challengers who want to join the group or breed the females. If another bull comes too close, the two begin to strut with a stiff-legged gait and eye each other with arched necks. If one bull is clearly larger, the other may back down but two bulls of equal size and determination could end up in a dramatic clash of wills. The confrontation begins as the bulls face each other and back up slowly, sweeping their heads from side to side. They may back up just a few feet or as much as 100 feet before they charge, slamming their armored skulls together with a resounding crack. Horn-to-horn shoving matches may follow and the jousting may be repeated more than a dozen times before one of the bulls gives up and runs away. While the battle rages, another bull may walk into the harem unchallenged and begin to court the females.

Bull muskox clash during the rut by ramming their armored skulls together.

Muskox have short legs and are not well-adapted to deep snow so they move to barren, wind-swept summits in winter. They may stay up to four months feeding very little but conserving their energy and living off their fat reserves. They turn their rumps to the wind in fierce storms and their dense woolen coats protect them in subzero temperatures.

Management

The Seward Peninsula has become a premiere destination for roadside muskox viewing but not everyone welcomes the animals' presence. Though muskox rarely charge people, they commonly charge and kill dogs. They have also been known to trample residents' traditional berry and wild greens picking sites and may compete with reindeer for good grazing range. At the time of transplanting muskox to the Seward Peninsula, wildlife managers sought little input from local Native villages but an ad-hoc group called the Seward Peninsula Muskox Cooperators has since been formed.

The group, including representatives from the region's villages and interested stakeholders, hears concerns, weighs the demands of hunting and wildlife viewing, and makes management recommendations to state and federal managers. Muskox herds are closely monitored by ADF&G with help from federal agencies (BLM, USFWS, NPS) to determine population status and acceptable levels of harvest through limited subsistence and trophy hunts.

Muskox can be trouble when they come too close to town.

Viewing tips

Use binoculars to scan ridge tops and high meadows in summer for dark spots on a hillside. On hot days check the river bottoms as well. The animals may appear docile, but they should not be approached. A protective bull or cow may charge.

A bear standing on its hind legs for a look around is usually curious, not threatening.

Grizzly bear

Grizzlies maintain enormous home ranges on the Seward Peninsula in their continuous search for food. Adult bears tend to be solitary except when they are mating in late May or early June and when sows are raising cubs. Two-year-old siblings often remain with their mother for several months after they are weaned but she will drive them away before the next breeding season. Grizzlies can range from dark brown to light blonde, with females tending to be lighter. Some bears are so light in color, they have been initially mistaken for polar bears.

Spring, summer, fall: The eating season

Grizzlies are voracious and opportunistic eaters, often seen in early spring feeding on plants and digging for roots and ground squirrels on snow-free slopes. They patrol the beaches for dead marine mammals that wash ashore. When the salmon are running, they move closer to rivers and lakes for protein-rich meals. Although grizzlies consume a great variety of plants and animals, berries are a vital part of their late summer diet when they are packing on lots of fat for winter hibernation. They may remain in the den without food or water for over six months.

Winter: The sleeping season

Whether bears are true hibernators is a matter of debate among scientists, but they certainly go into a suspended state. They don't defecate or urinate during this time but they are easily roused from their dens, especially a sow with cubs. Sows usually give birth in January while sleeping. The cubs, weighing less than a pound at birth, quietly nurse in the den. As the cubs grow larger in early spring, the sows grow restless and emerge from their dens.

Management

Human activity has shaped the region's grizzly populations over time. Gold miners, reindeer herders, federal predator control agents, and local residents kept their numbers low during the first half of the 20th century. But after statehood in 1959,

A sow and her three cubs resting.

Alaska began to promote grizzlies as trophy hunting animals. State wildlife managers reduced bear harvests in order to grow bigger bears—and they succeeded. Today, trophy grizzly bears are commonly harvested from the Nome road system.

Grizzlies often make an easy meal of moose calves and may kill as many as 90% of calves in a given area. ADF&G increased the legal bear harvest in recent years to try and boost the number of moose on the Seward Peninsula. Still, the region with its abundant berries and salmon continues to produce healthy bears. Sows with three cubs are not unusual and sows with four cubs, though rare, are reported more frequently than in many other parts of the state.

Viewing tips

Grizzly bears may be seen all along the Nome road system unlike black bears, which favor boreal forests, or the rare polar bear, which shows up along the coast after the spring sea ice has retreated. Grizzlies are especially drawn to marine mammal carcasses on the beach and spawning salmon streams. They are most active at dawn and dusk. Use binoculars to scan for bears at any good vantage point overlooking a combination of habitat types.

Wolf

Though rarely sighted, wolves are present in all seasons. They often feed on reindeer (or caribou) and moose, particularly in deep snow winters. Small mammals and fish supplement their diet in summer. Like grizzlies, they travel widely in an endless search for food and may be seen in any habitat. They are more active in late evening and early morning. They may travel 10 to 30 miles a day in winter.

Wolves are pack animals but may spread out in search of food.

Lynx are adept at climbing trees but hunt prey on the ground.

Lynx

The only wild cat present on the Seward Peninsula, lynx are abundant in years when their preferred prey, the snowshoe hare, is abundant. Lynx tend to be shy and unobtrusive but they have been seen on summer evenings when hares are grazing along the roadsides. They are known to prey on caribou and fox when hares are scarce.

Foxes (red and Arctic)

Red foxes are common in a wide array of habitats, searching for a meal of voles, ground squirrels, birds, bird eggs, berries, fish carcasses, or other carrion. They are more numerous when lemmings and voles are at a peak in their population cycles. Their color varies but the most common phase is a standard reddish-gold coat with black legs and feet and a white-tipped tail. A less common color phase is the "cross fox," which is brownish-yellow with a black muzzle and a dark stripe running across the shoulders and down the back.

White-furred Arctic foxes are less numerous. They may be found on the shore-fast ice feeding on the remains of a polar bear's kill, a marine mammal hunter's harvest, or discarded bait at people's crabbing holes. They are sometimes seen in the salt grass meadows of Safety Sound in summer as they wander widely to feed on birds nesting in the area.

A cross fox hunts for rodents on the tundra.

The short-tailed weasel is a very inquisitive animal and may emit a strong odor like a skunk if disturbed. Its fur is similar to the least weasel except that the short-tailed weasel has a black tip on the end of its tail.

River otters are graceful swimmers and fond of play. They can swim about six miles an hour and go faster for short distances by "porpoising" along the surface. They also dive to depths of at least 60 feet.

Weasels (ermine and least)

When small rodents are plentiful, so are ermine (short-tailed weasels) and the smaller least weasel. In summer both weasels have brown coats with yellowish white under-parts, and both turn white in winter. To distinguish between the two, look at the tail. The tip of the short-tailed weasel's tail is black year round while the least weasel's tail contains only a few black hairs.

Weasels are found in forested, brushy, and open country and build their nests in old buildings, lumber piles, rock slides, and stream banks. They must eat 40 percent or more of their body weight daily to survive and persistently hunt voles, small birds, fish, and insects. Weasels will boldly confront animals much larger than themselves. A severe winter with insufficient food is their worst enemy.

Wolverine, mink, marten, and river otter

These fur bearing animals are less commonly seen than their cousins in the weasel family. Mink and river otter are widely dispersed in low numbers throughout the road system and are most likely to be seen around rivers, streams, and ponds. Sightings of wolverine are especially rare though they are taken regularly by trappers during the winter. Marten are associated with the boreal forest and are found where this habitat occurs at the end of Council Road. They are similar to mink in color, size, and shape.

Marten are solitary creatures except during mating season around July and August.

Hares (snowshoe and Alaska)

Snowshoe hares are so named because of their large well-furred feet, which are suitable for soft, deep snow. Periodically abundant, they may be seen darting across the road or licking salts in the road bed. Other years none are seen. They are yellowish-brown in summer with a white underbelly and brown tail. In winter they turn white with a dusky undercoat and dark-tipped ears. They tend to live in shrubby areas, especially near the boreal forest. They eat mostly grasses, small plants, willow leaves, and wild berries. They are food for lynx, weasels, foxes, wolverines, large raptors, and owls.

A snowshoe hare is well camouflaged in its winter white pellage.

Alaska hares (or tundra hares) are found in higher and rockier tundra where they feed on willow shoots and other dwarf tundra plants. Like snowshoe hares, their numbers can fluctuate widely. Alaska hares are almost twice the size of snowshoe hares and, although they are also brown on top in summer, they always have a white tail. In winter they develop a long white coat and a white undercoat while the edges of their ears are blackish. Hares are locally called rabbits.

Porcupines use their large, sharp front teeth to satisfy an appetite for wood.

Porcupine

Porcupines are common in willows but well hidden unless spotted waddling across the road or a nearby meadow. Willow bark is their primary food but they may show up almost anywhere—from high rocky slopes to tundra meadows. The porcupine's only defense is deterrence. When it is alarmed and its quills are bristling, it also emits a pungent odor as warning. Once an animal has tangled with a porcupine, the memory of the painful experience and the smell will alert it next time. Porcupines stay active all winter.

Arctic ground squirrel

Arctic ground squirrels show how human modifications to the landscape can alter the range of wild animals. Having discovered that the loosened ground along road shoulders is good for burrow construction, Arctic ground squirrels are now common throughout the road system—not just in their typical habitat of dry, open, often rocky tundra. Like bears, they hibernate through the winter. Ground squirrels are called "parky squirrels" locally because their skins are used in traditional clothing. A few master skin-sewers still painstakingly stitch them into women's fancy parkas.

Arctic ground squirrel

Beaver

The beaver population has grown steadily on the Seward Peninsula, probably because of increased willow growth and because their numbers may have rebounded after heavy trapping and hunting in the early 1900s. Beaver have had a mixed influence on local salmon. Their dam construction can block streams, which has a negative impact on chum salmon migration, but the ponds they create provide additional nursery areas for young coho salmon.

Both active and inactive lodges can be viewed along the road system. Occupied lodges have freshly-cut branches incorporated into their structure, and in late summer and fall their winter food supply of willow branches will be evident in a partially-submerged cache in front of the lodge. Beavers have a wide, flat tail that they use to slap the water surface when startled or alarmed. They can swim long distances underwater to escape danger.

The beaver's heavy chestnut brown coat over a warm soft underfur keeps the animal comfortable in all temperatures. They groom their fur daily to keep it waterproof and frequently groom each other's fur.

The teeth of a beaver are adapted to the animal's tough woody diet. They grow continuously and the four incisors have a hard orange enamel covering in front.

Muskrat

This small mammal is often seen swimming in sloughs and ponds or hunched over on the banks chewing vegetation held in its front paws. Look for evidence of muskrat in marshy areas: vegetation and mud heaped two to three

A muskrat weighs two to four pounds and is much smaller than an adult beaver, which typically weighs 40 to 70 pounds.

feet high into summer feeding stations. After freeze-up, muskrats will deposit more plant material and mud over a hole in the ice and excavate a protected chamber inside the mound. This six to eight inch mounded area is called a "push-up" where they feed and rest away from the lodge. Harsh winters or overpopulation periodically lead to die-offs, and muskrat numbers fluctuate greatly. They are easily distinguished from beaver by their smaller size and rat-like tail. Muskrats construct slides and fairly well-defined channels through vegetation along stream banks and ponds.

Vole

Though rarely seen, these rodents are a primary protein source for raptors, owls, bears, wolves, foxes, mink, weasels, jaegers, and others. They are also some of the Arctic's toughest animals. They don't migrate, hibernate, or go into winter torpor. They just tough it out between the earth's warmth and the snow's insulation, feeding on the roots and seeds they spent the summer collecting and caching. Similar to mice but with small ears and short tails, they construct a network of tunnels under the insulating snowpack and live in tight groups to conserve body heat. They also burrow up through the snow to reach grass seed heads using various levels within the snow pack. After the snow melts, the remains of their extensive network of tunnels and half pipes may be visible.

Tundra voles are active throughout the winter and travel along a network of tunnels in the snow.

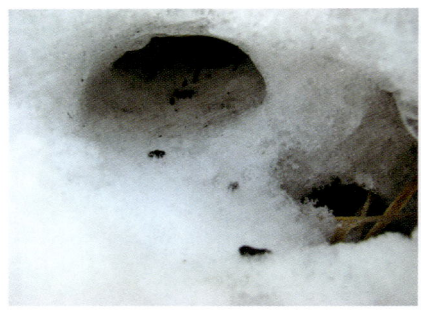

This vole tunnel is about an inch across (note scat outside the entry).

Lemming

Lemmings are similar to voles in many regards. Contrary to popular myth, they do not commit mass suicide—such is the power of Disney! Lemming populations, like those of voles, do fluctuate enormously, however, based on predators, food, climate, and other factors. Under ideal conditions, a population of lemmings may increase 10 times in a single year—keeping a host of larger predators well fed—but they will disperse or die off when they have exhausted their local food supply.

A collared lemming weighs about 14 ounces. In winter, two of its front toes enlarge and harden to form "scraper blades" under the claws, which are used for tunneling through the snow.

Shrew

The smallest mammal in Alaska has the biggest appetite and may be the most voracious predator. Every day throughout the year, a shrew needs to eat several times its body weight in insects, seeds, spiders, and carrion. With a heart rate of 700 beats a minute, a shrew will die if it goes more than a few hours without

Small mammals, like this shrew, are taken as prey by raptors hunting over tundra meadows.

eating. So it hunts for food continually, even attacking voles many more times its size. Shrews are not rodents but insectivores, related to moles, and they are one of earth's oldest mammals, dating back to the age of dinosaurs 100 million years ago. No one has conducted a shrew census in Alaska, but experts say there could be more than a billion of these fierce little predators.

Marine Mammals

Seals (ringed, bearded, spotted, and ribbon)

Ringed, bearded, spotted, and ribbon seals are collectively known as ice seals because they typically use sea ice as a clean and solid platform for birthing, nursing their pups, or resting after feeding. Ice seals are nutritional and culturally important to Native peoples throughout the Bering Strait region. Almost every part of the seal can be turned into a traditional Native delicacy and the omega-3 laden oil rendered from the blubber is a dietary staple. The tanned seal skin is a very useful leather that is used for equipment such as rifle cases and knife sheaths; clothing such as winter hats, parkas, and boots; and other traditional handicrafts such as Eskimo yo-yos, toys, and other items.

Ringed seal

Ringed seals are the smallest (~150 pounds) of the ice seals. Their fur has a distinctive pattern of many light gray rings around dark gray spots. They keep their breathing holes in the ice open by scratching away the constantly forming ice with their large, strong claws. They are often responsible for the scratch marks on the undersides of Styrofoam covers that are placed over winter crabbing holes to keep crab pot lines from freezing in place. They are the only Alaska seal to create under-ice lairs and do so in areas of rough heavy ice as shelter from winter storms and their main predator, the polar bear. During late spring ringed seals may be spotted sunning on top of sea ice by Cape Nome, Safety Sound, and even in front of Nome as they prepare to grow their annual new fur coat. In summer adult ringed seals typically follow the sea ice as it retreats north into the Arctic Ocean. Young seals may be seen during the summer months in areas of protected water such as lagoons—and even the Nome harbor.

Bearded seals are the largest (~600 pounds) of Alaska's ice seals. They are distinguished by their large body, relatively small head, and square-

Bearded seal

shaped front flippers. They are typically a uniform gray, although some may have a rusty color to their face and chest if they feed in areas with mineral-rich sediments. These large seals typically feed on clams, snails, crabs, flatfish, sculpin, and other small creatures that live on or near the seafloor. Adult bearded seals remain with the pack ice throughout the year, while younger bearded seals can be found in the waters of Norton Sound. The meat of the bearded seal is highly prized throughout northern and western Alaska. If you are lucky enough to eat Eskimo food in Nome, chances are—it's bearded seal. The seal's thick skin is used as strong leather for hand-sewn boot soles and rope. Further north the leather is used to cover smaller wood-framed skin boats.

Spotted seal

The medium-sized (~250 pounds) spotted seal has silver-colored fur covered with dark spots and is found further north than its close relative, the harbor seal. Spotted seals spend the winter along the leading edge of the pack ice with access to open water. Unlike most ice seals, however, they will rest on sandy beaches during ice-free months along the Bering and Chukchi Seas. Spotted seals feed on herring, capelin, and cod and are not afraid to follow these fish into near-shore waters and coastal lagoons. Spotted seals can be seen during the summer and fall in the ice-free waters of Norton Sound. If the water is calm, you may even see them in the shallow waters off the Nome beach. The bridge at Safety Sound and the Teller spit are good vantage points to view spotted seals feeding in the currents directly off the beach.

Ribbon seals, the rarest and most elusive of the ice seals, occur mainly in the Bering Sea. They are found in the open sea in summer and on the pack ice in winter. They average 5.5 feet long and 175 pounds.

Ribbon seal

Pacific Walrus

Walruses are typically not viewable from the Norton Sound mainland although they are abundant throughout the northern Bering Sea and Bering Strait region. They are very large (~2,500 pounds) and are distinguished by two ivory tusks (enlarged canine teeth) up to 36 inches in length. Both male and female walruses use their tusks for social display, to assist with climbing onto sea ice, and as a weapon against polar bears and killer whales. Walruses use the many sensitive whiskers (vibrissae) on their muzzle to search for soft foods on the sea floor. Walruses don't have sharp, biting teeth but instead use suction formed by pulling back a thick piston-like tongue inside their narrow mouth to slurp up their favorite foods such as sea worms, sea cucumbers, and clams. They are able to suck out the clams' soft parts, leaving the shells behind.

Pacific walrus

Preparing a walrus head mount requires first boiling it clean.

Walruses are an essential nutritional and cultural resource for coastal communities of the western Bering Strait region, especially those on the off-shore islands. They provide meat, organs, and blubber for much-loved Native foods. The extremely thick skin (1-inch thick) is specially processed into a pliable tough leather to cover the large wooden frames of the umiaq—a hand-crafted wooden framed boat—as well as for harpoon lines, rope, and many other items that require great strength and durability. The stomach, laboriously processed into a thin membrane, is used for the traditional Eskimo drums. Many Native peoples throughout the region supplement their subsistence lifestyle through the legal sale of handcrafted items that portray the wildlife, people, and spiritual heritage carved from walrus tusk ivory.

Beluga whale

Belugas are white, medium-sized (~12 feet in length), toothed whales that tend to travel in groups and use an extensive repertoire of whistles, grunts, and clicks to communicate, sometimes over long distances. Belugas are also adept at using echolocation (sonar) to navigate under the ice and find prey in murky waters.

A beluga whale ventures into shallow waters close to the Nome shoreline.

Some Bering Sea belugas travel more than 1,500 miles to spend their summers in Eastern Canada. Others have been known to travel up rivers following and feasting on migrating fish—even as far inland as Fairbanks. In the fall in Norton Sound, belugas are often seen from shore feeding on tomcod. Look for the white, finless back breaking the surface and the small spray from their blowhole as they breathe. Young belugas are small and typically light-gray in color. Belugas are regularly harvested by Native Alaskans. Beluga meat can be dried, fried, or frozen. The muktuk (skin with blubber attached) is eaten raw or boiled and is always shared with friends and family.

Gray whale

Gray whales are large whales (up to 45 feet in length) that spend their summers feeding in the rich marine waters of Alaska. They arrive in Norton Sound and the Bering Strait region from wintering areas near California at the end of spring. Traveling near shore during the spring and summer, gray whales feed by using their short cream-colored baleen to sieve small invertebrates from the silty

A gray whale calf displays the baleen it uses to filter its feed from seawater.

surface of the ocean floor. Gray whales are not typically seen from the Nome road system. If you are lucky enough to see a large whale at close range, look for the knuckle-like bumps in place of a dorsal fin along the ridge leading to the flukes. Traveling in a small airplane in the western Bering Strait region, you may see whale spouts and plumes of mud on the ocean's surface from gray whales feeding. Gray whales frequently have cyamid amphipods—or "whale lice"—and large barnacles that form large light-colored patches on their skin.

Harbor porpoise

The small-bodied (~5 feet in length) harbor porpoises travel quietly in small groups during the ice-free season. Often unnoticed, they barely disturb the waters as they surface to take a breath. On a calm day, look for their small dorsal

fin. These unobtrusive, blunt-nosed ocean dwellers can be found close to shore—even in lagoons and harbors—as they search for herring, capelin, and other foods that live in the shallow waters. Occasionally, they become entangled in local fishing nets.

Harbor porpoise

Killer whale

Killer whales are the largest (~25-30 feet in length) member of the dolphin family and occasionally seen off the Nome coastline during ice-free months. Look for the large (up to five-feet tall), distinctive dorsal fin breaking the surface and bold white markings on a black body. In the northern waters of the Bering Sea, killer whales typically travel in small pods and specialize in hunting marine mammals—from small seals to the largest whale—through coordination and skill. Coastal peoples have tremendous respect for the intelligence and skill of killer whales that visit the north.

The dorsal fins of killer whales are highly variable and used to identify individual whales.

Polar bear

Though rare, polar bears are occasionally spotted in the Nome area.

Iconic symbols of the Arctic, polar bears are powerful and patient predators on land, sea, and ice. Hundreds of thousands of years ago, the sea bear evolved from its brown bear ancestors to occupy an ecological niche in the frozen far north. Its white coat—made of water repellent hairs on top of a dense undercoat—serves as camouflage on the ice and reflects sunlight to the bear's black skin. Its large paddle-like feet, with their fur-covered pads, are well suited for swimming and for dispersing the weight of the bear when hunting on ice for ringed seal and other large prey. The fur on its feet also provides good traction in this slippery environment.

If you see a polar bear from the Nome road system, do not approach it. This species is a highly efficient and dangerous predator and has no fear of people. If public safety is a concern, immediately notify Alaska State Troopers. Alaska Natives may legally hunt polar bears, and the meat is a welcome and nutritious food source in many coastal communities. The hide/fur, teeth, and claws are often used to produce handicrafts and articles of clothing.

Steller sea lion

Steller sea lions are the largest sea lions in Alaska (adult males average 1,500 pounds) and these robust animals use the Bering Strait region during summer months as their feeding grounds. They will haulout on the rocky coasts of offshore islands to rest after feeding on seasonally abundant fish such as halibut, salmon, pollock, and cod. Occasionally, small numbers are seen on the rocks at Sledge Island, relatively close to Nome. Look for the large brown body, long front flippers, and massive head. Some Steller sea lions have numbers and letters branded on their left side as part of international research into the sea lion population decline in the North Pacific.

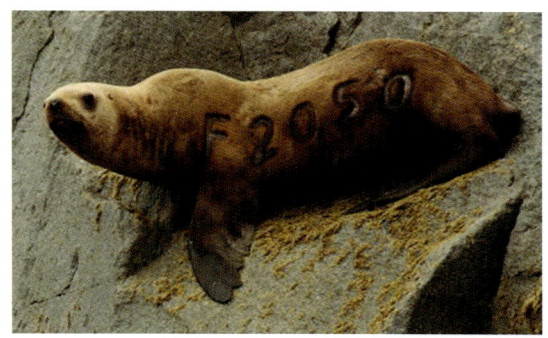

Report sightings of branded steller sea lions to any one of the appropriate agencies.

Note: If you see a sea lion with a brand, please record what you see and contact the UAF Northwest Marine Advisory Program Agent (443-2397) or the local ADF&G office (443-2271). If you find any stranded or dead marine mammal, please leave the animal undisturbed and call the MAP Agent, ADF&G, US Fish and Wildlife Service Law Enforcement Agent (443-2479), or Alaska State Wildlife Troopers (443-2429).

Ongoing Climate Change

For thousands of years, marine resources have sustained the Bering Sea Eskimo culture. Not surprisingly, coastal communities throughout the Bering Strait are deeply concerned with how the changing climate will affect the marine ecosystem, especially how the reduction of sea ice might affect the availability, accessibility, and general health of all marine mammals. With the region becoming sea ice-free for longer periods of time, some marine mammals are arriving earlier and staying later. Some marine species, like Atka mackerel and spiny king crab, are expanding their geographic range north to the Bering Strait, and Steller sea lions are becoming a more consistent and frequent visitor to Norton Sound and the Bering Strait region. It's uncertain how ice-dependent species will respond to changes in the ice extent and duration, but any significant environmental and ecological changes will be observed by coastal peoples and further test the resilience that has served them well as long-time residents of the Bering Strait region.

BIRDS

The Bering Strait region is a birder's delight. A combination of beaches, inland and ocean cliffs, lagoons, rivers, wetlands, meadows, tundra, fringes of forest, and mountains —all in close proximity— provide habitat options to an astounding diversity of bird species. More than 160 species of migratory birds follow flyways up both sides of the Pacific

Tundra swans

Ocean and across the Americas, Asia, and even Africa to breed, nest, feed, protect, and fledge their offspring. They join about two dozen resident species that tough out the long, dark, cold Arctic winters in interesting ways.

A female spectacled eider sits on the nest.

Birders often travel to Nome to check prized names on their life lists, species like bristle-thighed curlew, bluethroat, white wagtail, lesser sand-plover, and other Asian strays. Those who visit in late May and early June witness the enormity of the region's brief but riotous migratory period. With spring break-up advancing, any newly-budding willow shrub, quickly melting pond, and tangle of tussocks may harbor a bevy of birds, many displaying the vivid markings of their breeding plumage. By June birds are fully engaged in nesting. By August, however, the season is winding down as quickly as it began, and September's skies are filled with great noisy flocks of sandhill cranes and Canada geese and other migrating waterfowl.

Some birds are rare and elusive across their Seward Peninsula ranges, while others are quite common and easily seen. Almost all migrants, brilliant in their breeding colors, arrive in this avian mixing zone from North and South America or via more circuitous routes from wintering grounds in Asia and Africa. A small song bird called the northern wheatear winters on the savannas of northern and eastern Africa. Sensing that spring

Bluethroat

is approaching at its Alaska breeding grounds, the wheatear takes wing across much of Eurasia and arrives in Nome over the ice from the west. The bluethroat, found in North America only within the tundra regions of Alaska and the Yukon Territory, flies across the Bering Sea and Bering Strait from Southeast Asia, as does the Arctic warbler arriving from the Philippines.

Biologists aren't sure why some birds travel here from such distant lands but suspect their migration is tied to the Bering Land Bridge, also known as Beringia. During the Pleistocene ice age, lower sea levels exposed a swath of land—roughly 1,000 miles wide—which connected North America and Asia. Animals, including birds and humans, are believed to have migrated across this land corridor from the Old World to the New. When the glaciers melted and retreated, rising water levels covered the land bridge and created

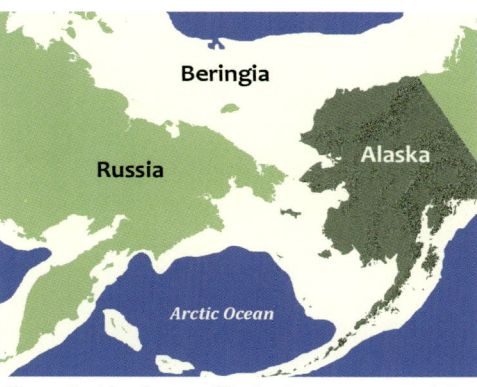

The ancient land mass of Beringia once connected the continents of Asia and North America.

the Bering Strait between Alaska and Siberia. Scientists believe birds, undaunted by the changes in land mass, continue to follow their ancient migration routes.

Bar-tailed godwits resting at Nome area beaches.

Some birds, such as the bar-tailed godwit, are distinguished by a phenomenal ability to fly non-stop over open ocean after departing Alaska for wintering grounds in the South Pacific. Studies show the godwit takes a direct route to New Zealand or eastern Australia and flies almost 7,000 miles without once stopping for food or water during its five-to-six day journey. In early fall these large shorebirds rapidly plump up their body mass, using pencil-thin bills to gorge on tiny clams in the Nome mudflats. They convert this fat into fuel, then burn protein (or muscle) for added energy on their long journey south.

Just as interesting as the migrants are the resident birds who become specialists in winter survival. Their internal furnaces are tuned to work efficiently and they know how to find the nourishment they need, no matter how limited the source. The black-capped chickadee has an amazing ability to rapidly convert food into fat, which fuels the bird during the long, cold nights of winter. Chickadees also cache food when plentiful, tucking seeds and other tasty bits into tree bark crevices and other hiding spots. Their tiny bird brains have good memories. They've been known to relocate the spot 45 days later even when it's covered in snow. Another resident bird, the American dipper—North America's only aquatic song bird—sticks close to upwelling springs, which are just warm enough to keep flowing all winter long. This bobbing bird feeds on insect larvae found on the river bottom.

An American dipper foraging (dipping) for aquatic insects. It often dips up to 60 times a minute.

Several raptors and predatory birds are residents too. Gyrfalcons, being ptarmigan specialists, are present in winter and become early season nesters. Occasionally, great horned owls or northern goshawks may reside where snowshoe hares

A golden eagle flying low in search of prey.

are abundant and ptarmigan are available as winter prey. The nomads of the north—the snowy owls—show up only when small mammals like lemmings and mice (microtines) are plentiful. Another bird, the northern shrike, will stay the course through the dark winter. This predatory songbird has earned the nickname 'butcher bird' from its habit of caching small mammal meals by impaling their carcasses on fence lines or branches, out of reach of ground predators. And no one can miss the ever-present, ever-vocal, and keenly observant common raven as it switches from omnivore to herbivore to predator to scavenger as the seasons cycle.

The powerful wing beat of a winter predator, a tiny brightly-colored rarity from a distant land, the short but intense drama of migration are all part of the excitement of birding at the crossroads of continents and oceans. Add to this an extensive and well-maintained road system during snow-free months and it's no wonder that birders flock to Nome.

Enthusiasts enjoy a grand day of birding in the Nome area.

Swans & Ducks

Common around small lakes and wetlands, the large, white-colored tundra swans can be surprisingly inconspicuous amid the shoreline vegetation. Bending their long graceful necks downward with tails pointed up, they can reach as far as three feet under water to feed on aquatic invertebrates and vegetation. Arriving in spring from wintering grounds in central California, breeding pairs of tundra swans

Tundra swans

head straight to their nesting grounds, often to the same nest year after year. Several hundred nonbreeding swans remain gathered throughout the summer at Safety Lagoon, eventually joined by the pairs and their new families as the fall migration period begins. Tundra swans are among the last waterfowl to migrate in the fall because the gray-plumed juveniles are not capable of sustained flight before late September.

Northern pintail (male, also called a drake)

Slim and long-necked, the northern pintail is the most common waterfowl that summers on the Seward Peninsula. The male is striking with his white neck, dark reddish-brown head, and long tail. Favoring shallow waters of coastal estuaries, these ducks dabble and tip-up for pond-weed seeds, sedges, grasses, and

Dabbling Ducks and Diving Ducks

Dabbling ducks, like the northern pintail, have short legs placed forward on their body, which enables them to spring vertically into flight from water or land with just a few wing beats. They feed on the water by dabbling at insects, seeds, and plants near the surface and by tipping-up their tails without diving as they reach for sub-emergent vegetation. Diving ducks, like the common eider, harlequin duck, and long-tailed duck, have longer legs set farther back on their body, which they use to propel themselves under water in pursuit of small fish. While agile underwater, they are awkward on land and need a running start on the water to become airborne.

aquatic plants. Northern pintails are early nesters, often arriving with the thawing of puddles throughout the month of May. Their numbers may surge locally when they are displaced by drought from nesting habitat in the Canadian prairies and the lower 48 states. Pintails typically winter in Washington, Oregon, California, Texas, Louisiana, and Mexico.

Common eiders (male) frequent coastal zones and marine waters.

The common eider is a large, stocky, colorful duck that frequents the coast where it breeds among ponds and lagoons. The male is conspicuous in his breeding plumage with a black crown, green nape, and white neck. Spring courtship is very intense with the male cooing somewhat like a domestic pigeon. The birds nest in dense colonies often at the previous years' site. A mother leading her young to water may be accompanied by non-breeding hens helping to protect the chicks. Many eiders overwinter on the coast where they molt in open water leads in pack ice. The common eider may live 20 years.

The harlequin duck is a medium-size sea duck that breeds on fast-moving streams and winters on rocky coastlines. Mated pairs are seen together on rivers until mid-June when the colorful male—splashed with rufous brown, dark blue, and white patterns—migrates to coastal waters and leaves the female to incubate the eggs. When the ducklings fledge in mid-August, they are frequently seen with their mother on rivers, feeding on invertebrates and small fish. Nicknamed the "sea mouse" for its distinctive squeaky call, the harlequin duck commonly winters in the Aleutians Islands.

The long-tailed duck, a black-and-white medium-size duck, typically breeds and nests in coastal areas adjacent to lagoons and river estuaries. At times the coastline is alive with their calls: a loud and repeated *aw-awoolee*. They fly low over the water's surface in bunched irregular flocks, alternately showing their white bellies and dark backs as they twist and turn in flight. The long-tailed duck is

A long-tailed duck (male) in courtship display.

one of the deepest diving ducks. Reaching depths of as much as 200 feet when foraging, it spends much more time underwater than above. The long-tailed duck has three distinct plumages each year throughout a series of partial overlapping molts. It winters on open ocean waters.

Ptarmigan

Alaska's official state bird, the willow ptarmigan uses camouflage against its many predators by changing from light brown in summer to snow white in winter. These stout, sociable birds have thickly-feathered feet, which insulate against the cold and help them "float" across the snow. They feed almost exclusively on willow buds and twigs in winter but supplement their diet with other plant leaves and berries in summer. When local roads are first plowed in spring, they frequent areas of exposed grit and gravel to replenish their gizzards.

Ptarmigan tracks lead in and out of a gravel pit where the birds come to fill their crops.

Rock ptarmigan

After the young hatch, the male assists in defending the chicks against gyrfalcon, snowy owls, red foxes, and other predators. The birds gather in large flocks in the fall. Later, they feed and roost clustered together in the snow.

Rock ptarmigan are found in the higher, rockier tundra slopes, feeding primarily on the buds and catkins of dwarf birch. In summer and fall they supplement their diet with leaves from a variety of plants, berries, and invertebrates. They are quite nomadic in winter with their movements affected by weather, snow conditions, and availability of food. Often, they mingle with willow ptarmigan and dig shallow bowls in the snow for protection from winter winds. The rock ptarmigan goes through similar color phases—though they occur a little later—and the males remain fully white until the breeding season is over. Both the willow and rock ptarmigan are year-round residents.

Loons

The red-throated loon is the smallest of the loons and the most commonly seen along the Nome roadways. Dark gray with a red throat in summer, the male engages in elaborate courtship or territorial displays that include bill-dipping, splash-diving, and fast underwater "rushing," where two birds charge each other at rapid speed. Unlike other loons, the red-throated loon can launch into flight without pattering—or running—a long distance to become airborne. As a result, they often nest on small ponds along coastal lowlands and may be seen heading out over coastal waters to catch fish for their chicks. The call of the red-throated loon includes a simple wail with varied pitches. Pacific loons can be found in both inland and coastal areas. They are stockier than the red-throated loon, show a gray nape and a black-and-white checkered back in summer plumage, and are extremely awkward when walking on land. Because of their body structure and size, Pacific loons require about 30 to 50 yards of open water to take flight, preferring to nest and feed on large, deep tundra lakes. The male builds the nest and assists with incubating the eggs and caring for the young. Both breeding and non-breeding birds may gather in large flocks to feed in coastal waters. The Pacific loon, like the red-throated loon, winters in Pacific coastal waters from southern Alaska to Baja, Mexico. Its calls may vary from a hoarse, repeated croak to a plaintive wail.

The chase is on.

Red-throated loons sparring. Male loons will fight—even unto death—over territories.

Raptors

The rough-legged hawk is widely distributed across the Seward Peninsula, though its numbers fluctuate greatly with the abundance of its primary prey: voles and lemmings. These large, soaring hawks—in both light-phase and dark-phase color morphs—arrive from their wintering grounds in the northwest United States and southern Canada when snow is still on the ground. They may re-use one of their old stick nests or build a new one on steep rocky outcrops overlooking tundra meadows. Perched among these outcroppings, they are on constant lookout for small rodents, ground squirrels, small birds, and ptarmigan. Buoyant in flight, they often hover over the hunting grounds, distinctive in their dark-tipped flight feathers and black-and-white banded tail pattern.

Rough-legged hawk

The adult golden eagle is a very large, dark bird with hawk-like proportions and a golden nape. It hunts mostly ptarmigan, squirrels, and hares while contouring the hillsides or soaring high above. Solitary and long-lived, golden eagles become breeders after four years and can live 25 years or more. They build the largest of the raptor nests, adding on sticks year after year. They also build alternate nests in the same area, which may be used by other raptors or ravens when not occupied by golden eagles. Most golden eagles migrate to the western United States and northern Mexico, but some overwinter on the Seward Peninsula.

A golden eagle readies to launch from its nest.

Nest rotation among cliff-nesting raptors and ravens

With every spring, a game of musical chairs begins among the various raptors and ravens that compete for cliff nest-sites found high above the Arctic tundra. Due to limited numbers of prime or favored cliff sites coupled with the early nesting habits of local birds, different species will often rotate through a single nesting area over successive breeding seasons. The first to choose nest sites are common ravens or gyrfalcons who may adopt the vacant stick nests built in previous years by golden eagles, rough-legged hawks, and ravens.

Golden eagles add a further layer of complexity by maintaining a cluster of alternate nest sites. Since eagles usually choose to occupy different nests through time, a gyrfalcon or peregrine falcon may use one of the eagles' empty sites or another species may move into the unoccupied nesting area and build their own nest near the empty eagle nest. Typically territorial and quarrelsome, the early nesters will ensure that late-arriving migrants are displaced to peripheral locations, causing them to nest at cliffs previously occupied by a different species.

The variation in nest sites selected by gyrfalcons, golden eagles, and ravens perpetuates a constant juggling of occupancy by other species, such as rough-legged hawks, peregrine falcons, and even Canada geese at some locations. Each year this jostling for prime real estate repeats itself as the nesting season progresses across the tundra.

The largest falcon in the world, the gyrfalcon (pronounced JER-falcon) is breathtakingly fast and powerful in flight. They prey mainly on ptarmigan, hares, and ground squirrels, but their diet includes a wide variety of other birds and small mammals. Somewhat blunt-winged for a falcon with a relatively long tail, most gyrfalcons on the Seward Peninsula are gray although plumage can range from dark gray to almost pure white. When not nesting in another species' stick nest, gyrfalcons build a scrape (a small cup-shaped depression to hold eggs) in the soil on a hard-to-reach cliff face. The female gyrfalcon regularly stores and caches prey in the vicinity of the nest. Banding and telemetry studies have shown that gyrfalcons travel between the Russian Far East and Alaska. They are year-round residents of the Seward Peninsula.

Gyrfalcon

Cranes

Every spring enormous flocks of sandhill cranes pass high over Nome's coastal flatlands headed for the Bering Strait and the Russian coastline beyond, but many pairs also break away to breed and raise their young on the Seward Peninsula. Tall gray birds with red foreheads and tufted rumps, they favor a mix of wetlands, ponds, and coastal river deltas to feed on berries, plant shoots and roots, insects, and small rodents. Walking on bended legs with their long necks stretched low over the ground, these large birds move about remarkably unnoticed in low vegetation. In the fall migrating flocks pass overhead again, but they are flying lower this time with birds often spiraling out of the sky to rest and feed before continuing on to Arizona, Texas, and northern Mexico. It's legal to hunt cranes in Alaska and they are considered a local delicacy in Nome.

Sandhill crane and chicks

Plovers

The American golden-plover is easily seen at its nesting grounds on dry tundra hilltops. Often skittering from point to point with a shrill *ku-wheep*, the plover stops to capture its prey with one or more pecks at the ground. These large shorebirds typically move to lower and wetter tundra areas after the young are born. As soon as the young are independent, the adults begin their migration to wintering grounds in South America. The juveniles may linger in flocks along coastal areas before beginning their migration in late summer.

A Pacific golden-plover is trying to distract attention away from its nest.

The Pacific golden-plover is very similar in appearance and behavior to the American golden-plover, indeed they were once considered the same species. However, the Pacific golden-plover prefers to breed and nest on lowland tundra slopes near the coast, and it winters in Hawaii, the South Pacific, and Southeast Asia. The two species also have different display calls and do not interbreed. Young plovers are able to run soon after hatching. They regularly forage near the nest while the adult continues to incubate late-hatching eggs.

Semipalmated plover

The semipalmated plover is found in upland areas along sandy gravel bars and lakeshores. If threatened while nesting, this small, boldly-patterned shorebird will attempt to lure an intruder away by pretending it has a broken wing. The bird feeds on small aquatic insects, crustaceans, and invertebrates. It has been known to swim short distances while foraging during migration. Most leave the area by early August and follow the Pacific coastline to wintering grounds from the central California coast to Chile.

Sandpipers, Phalaropes, and Allies

One of the rarest of the New World curlews and godwits, the bristle-thighed curlew is a prize sight for birders. The Seward Peninsula is one of only two areas where it breeds, the other being the extreme southern Nulato Hills—in the area east of the Yukon River delta. This robust shorebird has a long, downward-curved bill. While similar in appearance to the whimbrel, it is distinguished by its voice (a distinct whistle *chiu-eet* unlike the whimbrel's loud, rolling twitter), buffy-orange rump, and bristle-shaped feathers at the base of the leg. Nesting in areas of rolling tundra, it can be quite aggressive on

Bristle-thighed curlew

the breeding grounds. The bristle-thighed curlew begins moving out of the area in late June and early July to bulk up in pre-migration staging areas further down the coast. It feeds on invertebrates, carrion, rodents, and sea bird eggs—even using rocks to break open the eggs. The open ocean migration to islands in the South Pacific begins in earnest in late July and August.

Another large wading bird, the bar-tailed godwit sports a long, slightly upturned bill and a brick-red breast during the breeding season, which turns off-white in winter plumage. Breeding in open tundra on the Seward Peninsula, the godwit later flocks to protected coastal estuaries to fuel up on clams and worms for the long flight ahead. The bar-tailed godwit is distinguished by its southern migration, which is the longest non-stop migration of any bird. Using a satellite transmitter, scientists have tracked the Concorde-shaped bird on an eight-day flight of more than 7,000 miles from Alaska to New Zealand. The bird was clocked at speeds between 35 mph to 60 mph.

Western sandpipers are the most plentiful shorebirds on the Seward Peninsula. They nest in higher and drier tundra areas. As soon as the young can fly, the birds move to coastal wetland areas to feast on insect larvae found in shallow, muddy waters. Having bred and fed during the long summer days, these small sandpipers begin heading south in July for California, the West Indies, and northern South America.

Western sandpiper

Wilson's snipe

Wilson's snipe is often heard before it's seen. During the breeding season, males make long swooping dives in territorial displays, and the air rushing through their stiffened tail feathers creates a quick, repetitive, hooting noise called "winnowing" that announces their presence in the area. Arriving in mid-May to nest in tundra meadows, the male continues its acrobatic maneuvers until the chicks have hatched in early July. This small, stocky shorebird has an extremely long and flexible bill that it uses to probe the mud for small invertebrates. The bird is so well camouflaged that it is often not seen before it is flushed from grassy slopes or meadows.

The red-necked phalarope is a small, delicate shorebird frequently seen spinning in tight circles in small tundra ponds. Scientists believe the action of its lobed feet creates small whirlpools, which pull small aquatic insects and mosquito larvae to the surface. During the nesting season, male and female phalaropes reverse the typical avian sex roles. The female chooses the nest site, while the male builds the nest and cares for the eggs and young. The female is also more brightly-colored and aggressive than the male. The young grow quickly and they are on their own by the time they are two weeks old. These highly social birds flock together before their mid-summer migration. Though small, red-necked phalaropes are hardy, wintering at sea in the southern latitudes where they often feed on upwellings of plankton far from shore.

Gulls & Terns

Similar in appearance to the mew gull, black-legged kittiwakes are found in coastal colonies on rocky headlands and sea cliffs. They primarily eat small fish in coastal waters, sometimes traveling as far as 40 miles from their nesting cliff sites to feed. Breeding success and the overall numbers in a colony follow a boom-and-bust cycle that depends on seasonal concentrations of fish within feeding range.

Black-legged kittiwakes

Black-legged kittiwakes winter in the open seas of the North Pacific Ocean and the southern Bering Sea, then move north with the retreating sea ice in spring.

Mew gull

One of the smallest of the white-headed gulls, the mew gull typically nests inland among wet tundra meadows with ponds, lakes, or rivers. Nonbreeders stick to coastal zones where they cluster and rest on beaches and the edges of lagoons and ponds. After breeding, large flocks of adults may gather on mud and sand flats at the mouths of larger rivers. They typically feed on small invertebrates and fishes but, given the opportunity, they will also eat young birds, berries, carrion, and garbage. They winter from Prince William Sound on down the California coastline.

The huge glaucous gull breeds across most of the high Arctic. It winters farther north than most gulls but also turns up as far south as California and Virginia. An active predator at seabird-nesting colonies, the gull will walk into colonies and take eggs and chicks left unprotected. The glaucous gull breeds along marine and freshwater coasts, tundra, offshore islands, cliffs, shorelines, and ice edges. It winters along maritime coasts, freshwater lakes, agricultural fields, urban areas, and garbage dumps.

The Aleutian tern is distinguished from the Arctic tern by a black bill and a white bar across the forehead of its black-capped head. But the differences extend beyond just looks. The Aleutian tern spends winters at sea in the North Pacific. It nests only in coastal lowlands, particularly in small colonies around Safety Lagoon. Later in the summer, flocks of Aleutian and Arctic terns may mix.

Aleutian terns

Arctic terns: juvenile (l) and adult (r)

A small slender gray-white bird with a black cap and red bill, the Arctic tern travels 10,000 miles from the Antarctic ice edge to breed and raise its young on the Seward Peninsula each summer. Though widely distributed, the birds are most abundant in wet tundra meadows and ponds close to the coast. They are frequently seen swooping and diving into both saltwater and freshwater for small fish and invertebrates. By late July flocks of terns may begin to gather along the coast. Their long-distance migration is underway by mid-August.

Jaegers

Often seen in flight or hovering over the tundra in search of prey or carrion, the long-tailed jaeger is rarely seen outside of its Arctic breeding grounds because it spends over three-quarters of its life at sea. A spot of white in rolling tundra meadow is often a jaeger perched on a nest or small rise. Of

Long-tailed jaeger

the three jaegers, the long-tailed jaeger is the smallest, the most abundant and widely-distributed in the Arctic, and breeds the farthest north. It will harry gulls to steal their food but usually feeds by catching fish and insects. Lemmings and voles are staple foods on the breeding grounds, and the long-tailed jaeger does not breed at all in years when rodents are scarce.

Murres and puffins

The thick-billed murre is found in Arctic waters across the globe, living along the edges of pack ice in winter. One of the deepest diving birds (regularly descending to depths of more than 300 feet), it uses its wings to swim underwater in search of fish and invertebrate prey. The thick-billed murre nests in colonies on steep cliffs, shifting pebbles or other debris on a rocky ledge where it lays the eggs. These fragments, held together by feces, may serve to protect the eggs from rolling off the ledge.

Thick-billed murres

Horned puffin

The horned puffin dives underwater to capture prey, pumping its wings to propel itself forward. It can dive up to depths of 80 feet to catch its prey. Nesting in coastal colonies on rock crevices and cliffs, this striking seabird spends the rest of the year in the northern Pacific. The horned puffin delivers small fish to its nestlings, carrying them crosswise in its bill. One was even observed carrying 65 small fish at once. The bird sheds its showy bill ornament in winter.

Owls

The short-eared owl is the most common owl found along the Nome road system, but its numbers vary widely depending on the availability of voles and lemmings. A medium-size mottled-brown bird with a large round head, it flies close to the ground in rocking, buoyant flight in search of prey. The owls typically arrive from the Lower 48 in early May and nest in grassy hummocks of open tundra meadows if prey is abundant. If scarce, they will quickly move on.

Short-eared owl

Corvids

Their high intelligence and penchant for eating trash and stealing fish from drying racks make common raven both a delight and an annoyance. Ravens often build their nests on man-made structures such as dredges, cabin roofs, bridge supports, and even the white, golf ball-shaped weather radar station on the Kougarok Road. They also build stick nests on rock cliffs and sometimes nest in cottonwoods. Opportunistic eaters, ravens feed on a wide range of items, including the eggs of other birds, spawned-out salmon, small mammals, carrion, and berries. Many tough out Nome's long, cold, windy winters by hanging out at the landfill, dubbed the Raven Haven.

Common raven

Swallows

Shiny blue-green backed birds with white underparts, tree swallows often nest in the cottonwoods around Pilgrim Hot Springs and in the nest boxes placed near homes and camps. Like other swallows, these birds are in constant flight as they capture and forage on mosquitoes and other flying insects. When not breeding, the birds congregate in enormous flocks and night roosts. The tree swallow winters farther north than any other American swallow and returns to its nesting grounds long before the other swallows.

Bank swallows build their nests in river silt banks.

Small, slender, and long-winged with a brown back and white underbelly, bank swallows nest by excavating burrows in the silty soils above the high water level along river-cut banks. They also populate human-made sites, such as sand and gravel quarries or road cuts where vertical soil banks are present.

Small, stocky, and long-winged with a blue-black crown and back and a square tail, cliff swallows often build their gourd-shaped mud nests under bridges where they are seen darting and soaring over the water in pursuit of airborne insects. These gregarious birds nest in large colonies.

A cliff swallow gathers mud to build a nest.

Dippers

The American dipper is a chunky, dark gray, plain bird with an extraordinary ability to walk underwater using the current to stay submerged as it searches for stream-dwelling prey. North America's only aquatic songbird, American dippers are year-round residents on the Seward Peninsula. They stick close to spring-fed open waters in winter. The bird's low metabolic rate, extra oxygen-carrying capacity of its blood, and a thick coat of feathers help it to withstand the cold water temperatures.

The hungry mouths of American dipper chicks.

Leaf Warblers

A small, drab-colored bird, the Arctic warbler is the only Old World warbler with a foothold in North America where it breeds in Alaska. The earliest spring migrants arrive in late May. It usually nests in stands of medium-height willow, often along streams. The bird's constant wing-flicking while foraging may be a way of flushing prey. The Arctic warbler winters in Southeast Asia, most commonly in the Phillipines.

Arctic warbler

Thrushes

The bluethroat, a small, brown thrush with a bright blue and rust-red throat, is highly sought after by serious birdwatchers. Spending winters in Southeast Asia where it is more widespread, the bluethroat breeds in limited areas in northwestern Alaska. Normally very secretive, it is typically found in limited numbers where low shrub thickets are associated with water courses and swales on lowland slopes. It is most easily observed when singing or performing flight displays. In the open, it often jerks up its tail and fans it for a quick flash of rufous patches at the base.

Bluethroat

Northern wheatear chick

The northern wheatear returns yearly to the Seward Peninsula from the savannas of northern and eastern Africa. It is often seen on rocky tundra slopes at higher elevations where it is identified by the flash of its distinctive tail, which is white with bold, black outer bands. This dapper sparrow-sized bird flits from rock to rock, fanning its tail and bobbing. The male defends its territory by singing, often imitating other birds.

Of all the American spotted thrushes, the gray-cheeked thrush has the most northern breeding range. A medium-sized brownish-gray thrush, this shy skulker of the thick shrub zones and underbrush is infrequently seen. Its song is a distant-sounding series of flute-like tones that rise and fall in pitch.

Wagtails

A small olive-colored songbird with yellow underparts, the eastern yellow wagtail inhabits open country near water, wet meadows, lakeshores, and riverbanks. Its call is a high pitched *jeet* that announces the bird's presence when disturbed. The bird winters in Eurasia.

Eastern yellow wagtail

Longspurs and Buntings

For many visitors who have only seen Lapland longspurs in their dull winter plumage, it's a treat to see the tuneful adult males with their distinctively black throat and rust-red back of the neck. The Lapland longspur is named for the exceptionally elongated, black-colored claw of its hind toe.

Even with temperatures dipping well below 0°F and snow covering most of the ground, the male snow bunting returns to its Seward Peninsula breeding grounds every year in early April, about four to six weeks before the female. He uses this time to pick out and defend a good nesting site but still flocks with other snow buntings

Snow bunting family

to forage and roost in loose groups of 30 to 80 birds. Though mostly white, this species of bunting has black markings on its back and tail and large black bills, legs, and feet.

McKay's bunting

McKay's bunting winters on the western coast of Alaska and nearby islands. Large numbers are attracted to uncovered stems of beach rye in Nome area snowscapes and to the feeders maintained by local residents. In spring they move to breeding grounds on Hall and Saint Matthew Islands in the Bering Sea. Though closely resembling the snow bunting, McKay's bunting is much whiter overall and a true northern 'snow bird'.

Wood Warblers

With the most uniformly yellow-colored plumage of any warbler species, the yellow warbler is often found in medium and tall willows capturing insects by gleaning, flycatching, and hovering. Its song is a bright **sweet-sweet-sweet-sweeter-than-sweet**. It winters in the tropics.

Widespread in willow and alder thickets, the Wilson's warbler is easily identified by its yellow underparts, black cap, and olive-green back. It picks insects from foliage and twigs, hovers to pick prey from leaves, and snatches insects from the air. In early summer the foraging male utters long bursts of vivid song.

Yellow warbler

Sparrows

A small brown sparrow with brown streaks on its white underparts and yellow coloration above its eyes, the savannah sparrow is commonly found in open tundra meadows and salt marshes. When flushed, it may fly high to its next perch or drop to the ground and dart away.

Savannah sparrow

A large sparrow with bold stripes and a heavily-streaked chest, the fox sparrow has a lively, loud, ringing whistle. It is abundant in dense shrub habitats. When feeding on the ground, the fox sparrow scratches so vigorously to uncover food that it often sounds like a much larger animal.

The white-crowned sparrow is easy to identify with its smart black-and-white head, pale beak, and gray breast. The bird tends to stay low at the edges of brushy habitat, hopping on the ground or on branches usually below waist level. Listen for its thin, sweet whistle.

White-crowned sparrow

Blackbirds

Marked by its conspicuous yellow eyes, the rusty blackbird feeds at the shrubby edges of ponds by walking and flipping over leaves and debris to find aquatic insects. At the end of summer prior to migration, flocks of these birds frequent willow thickets near rivers in coastal areas and supplement their diets with berries.

Finches

The common redpoll is a small brown and gray finch with a rosy chest and red cap that is abundant year-round in open subarctic areas and northern forests. These tiny birds are known to survive extremely cold temperatures and have adapted to harsh winter conditions in a number of ways. They have very fluffy body feathers, even sporting feathers on areas of the body that are bare in most other birds. During long Arctic

Common redpoll

nights, they often roost in snow tunnels to preserve body heat. The hoary redpoll tends to be paler than the common redpoll, but it is often difficult to distinguish without observing the distinctive white rump field mark of this species.

FISH

Salmon

All five species of Pacific salmon are found in waterways on the Seward Peninsula and are the fuel that powers much of the ecosystem. Salmon runs, numbering from thousands to millions of fish, pump protein and nutrients throughout a network of rivers and streams as they journey upstream to spawn and die. Residents fill their freezers with fresh-caught salmon and cut and hang them to dry on racks at fish camps and homes.

Salmon leave the ocean and travel back to their natal waters to spawn.

A grizzly fishes the river for salmon.

Bears snag passing salmon for a burst of high-quality protein. Other fish eat the translucent red eggs, while an array of small mammals, fish, and birds gobble down the young salmon fingerlings as they make their way to sea. Even the spawned-out carcasses provide food for scavengers. The nutrients released as they decay also nourish vegetative and aquatic life to provide food back up the chain.

What's in a name?

Each of the five species of Pacific salmon has at least two different names, not even counting their scientific names. Chinook may be called king, tyee, or blackmouth salmon and chums are also known as dog, keta, or calico salmon. Sockeyes are also called reds, cohos are silvers, and pinks are humpies. Salmon eggs and just-hatched salmon (at left) are called salmon roe and alevin.

Chum salmon are found in almost all the drainages that flow into Norton Sound. A preferred subsistence catch, they are gutted, split, and hung to air-dry on racks. In the late 1990s, severe declines in the chum runs created hardships for

many families and triggered fishing restrictions. The runs experienced a rebound in the 2000s, which allowed for a higher—though still regulated—subsistence take in the Nome area.

Adult chum usually enter rivers and streams in late June to early July, spawning in August. The young emerge the next June and head directly for salt water. They remain at sea for three to five years before returning as adults to spawn and die.

Harvesting chum and sockeye with a beach seine net.

Pink salmon are the most abundant salmon in road-accessible waters, and their small size (2-4 pounds) makes them desirable for traditional cutting and hanging because they dry faster. Pinks have stronger runs on alternate years—up to ten times larger than the preceding year. In high run years, which can number over one million in numerous Nome area rivers, you may see pinks offshore leaping into the air before entering fresh water.

Pink salmon drying on the rack.

Pinks enter streams from late June to early July and spawn in July and August. Young fish emerge the next spring and travel directly to the sea. They remain one year before returning to spawn, completing their life cycle in two years.

Sockeye salmon spawn in lakes and have been found in large numbers only in the Pilgrim River where they are bound for Salmon Lake and in the Sinuk River where they are bound for Glacial Lake. The Salmon Lake population has suffered from overharvesting since a road built in the 1950s has allowed easy access to the lake. Efforts to restore the population, including fishing restrictions and

Sockeyes, still a bright silver, begin to head upriver.

habitat restoration, have met with varied success in recent years with record runs beginning in the mid-2000s, a population crash in 2009 and 2010, and a slight rebound in 2011.

Coho spawn in most Seward Peninsula rivers but they arrive after the warmer, sunnier days of summer are past. As a result, they are less suitable for drying on traditional fish racks. Anglers eagerly anticipate their arrival, however, because coho are feisty when landed with a rod and reel—and they taste good.

Salmon go through a dramatic transformation on their way up river to spawn. The top photo is a coho before it has entered the river, the bottom photo is a spawning coho.

Coho salmon tend to spawn at night.

Adult coho enter area streams and rivers from late July through early September, with runs peaking in the latter half of August. Spawning occurs from mid-September through October. Young coho emerge the next spring and spend one to two years fattening up—often on pink and chum salmon fry—in freshwater ponds and beaver sloughs before heading for salt water. They remain at sea for only one year, returning to spawn as three- or four-year-olds.

Chinook salmon are not abundant on the Seward Peninsula where they return in very small numbers in the major rivers. Larger runs of only a few hundred fish are found in Fish River and Pilgrim River.

Adults first enter the rivers in late June or in July and spawn in July and August. Young fish emerge the following June and usually remain in fresh water for one to two years before traveling to the sea. After three to five years at sea, they return to spawn and die.

Nutrients released from rotting salmon carcasses provide nourishment back up the food chain.

Non-salmon species

Arctic grayling are found in most Seward Peninsula rivers. They spawn in spring and the young emerge from the streambed two to four weeks later. In the Nome area, Arctic grayling grow rapidly on a diet of small fish, insects, mice, and other available food for seven or eight years until they have achieved sexual maturity and about 15 inches in length. After spawning for the first time, they

Arctic grayling, part of the salmon family, is a sportfish superstar.

continue to grow more slowly. Arctic grayling can live for 30 years. The state record, weighing 5 pounds 2 ounces, was caught in the Fish River drainage in 2008, and fish over 2 pounds are common in many roadside streams. Because populations in many roadside rivers and streams are small, it is easy to overfish Arctic grayling in western Alaska. Daily sport fishing bag and possession limits are designed to keep harvests low while still providing opportunities to catch large fish. Both the Nome River and Solomon River are closed to Arctic grayling fishing.

Dolly Varden char (known locally as trout) spawn in fresh water streams in the fall. The young emerge the following spring and remain in fresh water for two or three years until they are about six inches long and ready to begin their annual spring migration to the sea. There they feed until August or November when

they return to overwinter in freshwater. They migrate two or three times before returning to their home river in September or October to spawn for the first time. Unlike Pacific salmon, Dolly Varden live to spawn several seasons, usually every other year once they have reached maturity. In non-spawning years, they may overwinter in rivers other than their home rivers. They develop brightly-colored bodies and fins when

The Dolly Varden char is named after a character in a Charles Dickens novel.

spawning, and males tend to develop a hooked-jaw (called a kype), similar to a spawning salmon. A typical Dolly Varden caught on the Seward Peninsula averages 1 to 3 pounds but can weigh up to 7 pounds, while Dolly Varden found in the Kotzebue drainages to the north can weigh over 15 pounds.

Arctic char are often confused with Dolly Varden but, on the Seward Peninsula, they are only found in remote land-locked lakes in the Kigluaik and Bendeleben

Mountains. They entered these lakes before uplifting and streambed erosion isolated them. They continued to breed in genetic isolation and recent genetic testing has shown that each lake's char has unique characteristics not found in the other lakes' fish.

Arctic char are confined to isolated land-locked lakes in the area.

Northern pike are found mostly in the lower Pilgrim and Kuzitrin Rivers, the Fish River drainage, and other drainages of the Imuruk Basin. They typically favor slow-moving waters and weedy, backwater sloughs. Northern pike spawn

in the spring and their young are actively swimming and feeding within two weeks. A predatory species that primarily eats other fish (generally whitefish but also juvenile salmon, Arctic grayling, and other northern pike), they have also been known to eat voles, muskrats, and small ducks. Pike can grow to over 20 pounds on the Seward Peninsula and, despite their many bones, are excellent table fare. Some people travel to pike areas in winter by snowmachine and fish for them through a hole in the ice.

Northern pike are ambush predators, hence their camouflage coloring.

Burbot—the only freshwater cod—occur in many Seward Peninsula waters, preying almost exclusively on other fish. They are usually found in the lower reaches of rivers.

Also called lush or lingcod, burbot migrate up the Fish River to spawn in late November and December where willow weirs were once deployed in the ice for subsistence catches on the Niukluk River below Council and the Fish River above White Mountain. They were once an important food source for the area around Pilgrim Hot Springs and Mary's Igloo.

Freshwater burbot

Six different species of **whitefish** are found in Seward Peninsula waters. Most live in fresh and/or brackish water and feed on plankton, small clams, snails, and aquatic insects. The least cisco is the smallest of the six. The round whitefish is larger but more variable in size and occasionally caught when fishing for Arctic grayling. The humpback whitefish, which can reach 24 inches, is occasionally caught during sport fishing. The most sought after is the broad whitefish, the largest of the six (they can reach 5-6 pounds), which is prized as a food fish by some. Broad whitefish are seldom caught by rod and reel, but people seine for them late in the fall or spear them through holes cut through river ice. The Bering cisco is the only whitefish on the Seward Peninsula known to migrate to the sea. Sometimes found in brackish lagoons, they are not known to spawn on the Seward Peninsula. Sheefish are also found in waterways on the peninsula.

Whitefish are an important subsistence food for residents of the Seward Peninsula.

Blackfish have a unique ability to tolerate low levels of oxygen and even light freezing. This allows them to inhabit small ponds and lakes that are not frozen to the bottom but where other fish cannot survive. Schools of these small mud-colored fish, which rarely exceed 8 inches in length, are sometimes viewed through clear pond ice just after freeze-up. If stranded temporarily in wet tundra during summer dry spells, blackfish can absorb oxygen from the air. They are a favorite food of otter, mink, and Arctic grayling.

Red king crab caught off the Nome coast tend to be smaller than their cousins to the south but are much prized for their sweet meat. Blue king crab is more common near King Island. Local residents fish for crab either with hand lines or crab pots in the winter before the ice goes out or with rakes in the spring when the crab come in close to shore to breed. King crab have been spotted walking on the beaches of Safety Sound.

Fishing for king crab is a popular winter activity.

Halibut tend to stay several miles off-shore and roam across huge areas of the ocean floor in search of food. This makes fishing for halibut challenging in the Nome area.

Historically, **capelin** is an important subsistence fish with a spawning run in June. Some years these small fish are so prolific that residents—out fishing at dusk and low tide—use trash cans to dip for them. They are also an important forage fish for salmon, birds, and marine mammals.

Capelin are important food for other fish, birds, and humans.

Capelin spawn on sandy beaches two weeks after herring spawn on rocky seaweed-covered areas. The male capelins have two fuzzy strips on each side while the females are smooth and shiny. Two males will sandwich a female—the fuzzy strips help them position themselves—and they spawn as a threesome. They are also called candlefish because they burn like a sooty candle when dried.

Herring are common in the Nome area during a spawning migration in early June and an exit migration in mid-September. Generally caught with gill nets by commercial or subsistence fishermen, herring can be seen spawning on eel grass in Safety Sound or on the Nome port jetty in June, about a week after the ice is out.

Saffron cod (tom cod) are present year-round and used as human food, crab bait, and dog food, much like the white fish caught at ice-up on the Kuzitrin River. Commonly caught as the lagoons and estuaries freeze in October, they school near the entrances to Safety Sound as masses of gulls wheel overhead. Beach seiners using dog mushing teams to pull the nets have caught as many as twenty-five 55-gallon drums of cod in one set. Three to five drums full is normal. As the ice hardens, people jig or dip them from estuaries in about five feet of water—often catching a few rainbow smelt as well—usually around the Nome River, Snake River, or near the Solomon River/ Bonanza Channel Bridge.

Nome residents ice fishing for tom cod at the small boat harbor.

MILEPOST
to the Nome
Area Roadways

This section features three main roads originating out of Nome, as well as a walking tour of birding hot spots in town. Shorter roads and side roads in the area and other locations around town also hold wildlife viewing potential. Follow the road tips below to improve your travel and safety on Nome's gravel roads.

Check road conditions before you go. For information on road conditions and closures, contact the Alaska State Troopers at (800) 443-2835 or the Alaska Department of Transportation at (907) 443-3444.

Keep your eyes on the road. Pull over to look for wildlife.

Check behind you before you hit the brakes and pull off the road to stop. Another car may appear over a rise or around a bend without notice.

Keep to your side. The roads are narrow and often have soft shoulders, so please don't take your half out of the middle.

Small hills can cause big problems. Stay to the outside of the road when approaching a small rise. It's difficult to see if an approaching car is driving in the middle of the road. Avoid stopping on the back side of a small rise.

Close the door. If you get out of your vehicle, close doors that open to the road.

No need to eat dust. A vehicle ahead can kick up a long dust trail on a dry day. Slow down, relax, and enjoy the view until your visibility improves. You may want to roll up your window when a car passes in the other direction.

Avoid parking on bridges. Look for wide shoulders or pull-outs near bridges.

Carry a spare tire and tools. The roads are generally well-maintained but are gravel and flat tires do happen.

Fair warning

Consider polarized sunglasses. The northern sun generally travels in a low-angled arc across the horizon. Polarized sunglasses can cut glare and make driving safer.

Carry everything you will need. There are no roadside services. Fill your gas tank before you leave Nome!

You may be able to purchase gas from the Teller Native Corporation, but don't rely on it. Carry food, water, toilet paper (and a bag to collect used toilet paper and trash), and other necessary personal items.

Be prepared for limited communications. Only Teller and Nome have phone service and cell phones have limited, if any, range on the Seward Peninsula. Satellite phones generally work.

Tell someone where you are going and when you plan to return. You can provide your travel plans to the Alaska State Troopers or the Nome Police Department. Please be sure to check in when you return.

Respect private property. The many cabins and small settlements along the road system are private subsistence and recreation camps. Do not trespass or interfere with activities.

Stay alert when you leave the car. Watch for bears and other animals that may be nearby. Be aware that rain and other factors can dramatically change water levels in streams and rivers. Check if stream banks are stable before approaching.

Your vehicle can serve as a blind from which to view and photograph wildlife safely.

Don't hike unless prepared for wilderness hiking. Tundra areas may look like easy walking but soft ground and hidden swales can be challenging. Despite the open vistas, it is easy to lose your way in the rolling landscape.

Key to the Milepost

Mile 0 to 7 | Nome to Snake River

This top level category names a section of the road and gives general information about the countryside and other features along this segment of the road.

Habitat: River Valley

This level of the key lists the habitat types found along the broad sections of road indexed above. Check the habitat section earlier in the book to learn more about the natural environments used by wildlife.

▶ Mile 2.8: Dexter Bypass Road

Listings at this level give road milepost and a local name or feature. In many cases mileposts are approximate because many of the green and white highway markers are missing and sections of the road have been re-routed during maintenance and improvements. The distance between markers is not always exact, but they are the best point of reference. Several side trips are also listed, but be aware that roads may be poorly maintained and help not readily available.

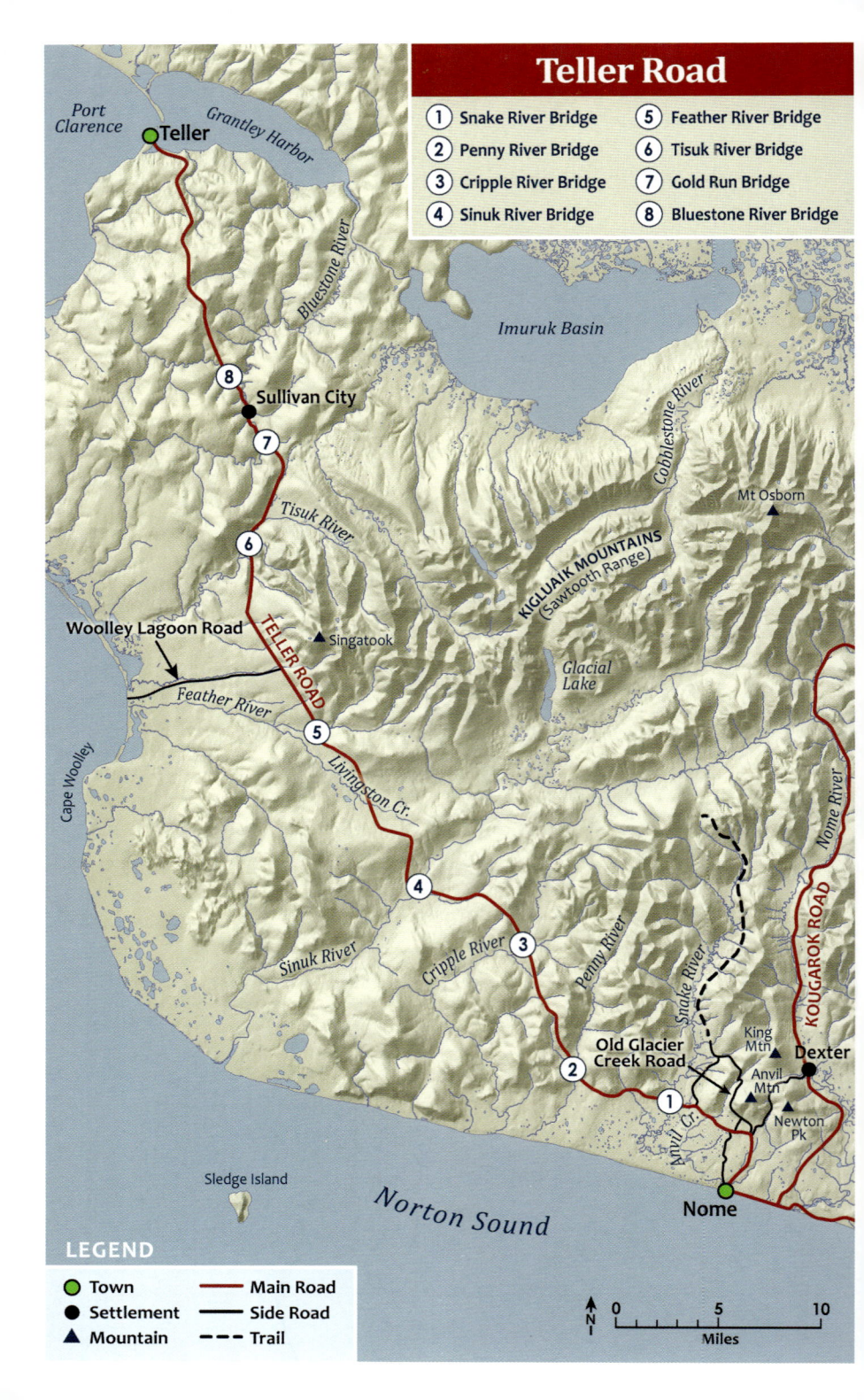

Teller Road

1. Snake River Bridge
2. Penny River Bridge
3. Cripple River Bridge
4. Sinuk River Bridge
5. Feather River Bridge
6. Tisuk River Bridge
7. Gold Run Bridge
8. Bluestone River Bridge

Port Clarence

Grantley Harbor

Teller

Bluestone River

Imuruk Basin

Sullivan City

Cobblestone River

Mt Osborn

Tisuk River

KIGLUAIK MOUNTAINS (Sawtooth Range)

Woolley Lagoon Road

TELLER ROAD

Singatook

Glacial Lake

Feather River

Cape Woolley

Livingston Cr.

Nome River

Sinuk River

Cripple River

Penny River

Snake River

KOUGAROK ROAD

Old Glacier Creek Road

King Mtn

Anvil Mtn

Dexter

Newton Pk

Sledge Island

Anvil Cr.

Norton Sound

Nome

LEGEND

- 🟢 Town
- ⚫ Settlement
- 🔺 Mountain
- ━━ Main Road
- ── Side Road
- - - - Trail

N

0   5   10

Miles

Teller Road

Muskox are often seen along Teller Road. During the breeding season, they congregate in herds of females and subadults (like those pictured above) and a single dominant bull.

This road is officially named the Bob Blodgett Nome-Teller Highway after an early lawmaker from Teller, but most people call it the Teller Road. Though gravel, the road is well-maintained and runs 72 miles northwest from Nome to the Inupiat village of Teller, located at the base of the sand spit that divides Port Clarence and Grantley Harbor.

Traversing rolling upland tundra meadows with many creek and river crossings, the road skirts the western flank of the rugged, glacier-carved Kigluaik Mountains. In good weather, this road offers stunning views of the mountains, also called the "Kigs" or Sawtooth Range. The Bering Sea is to the west of the highway route. On particularly clear days, you can see King Island 40 miles offshore. The road also leads through some of the country's earliest gold mining areas.

Gas service in Teller is unreliable so be sure to leave Nome with a full tank. Several village stores carry a limited selection of food and local crafts.

Mile 0 to 7 | Nome to Snake River Bridge

Habitat: Side slopes, tundra meadow, wet tundra, ponds

The lowland tundra close to the coast is dotted with many ponds of varying sizes due to the poor drainage that results when level terrain is underlain by frozen soils. Places with contour and hints of elevation are related to beach gravels deposited in geologic

Fresh tracks on the riverbank indicate a moose has passed by recently.

times when ocean levels were much higher. The wet meadows give way to significant areas of placer mining of gold bearing gravels, especially in the vicinity of Nome. This section of highway crosses habitats that are used by moose, muskox, reindeer, and birdlife linked to wet meadow environments, such as American wigeon, northern pintail, green-wing teal, and red-necked phalarope.

▶ Mile 0 to 3: Anvil Mountain and White Alice antennas

For the first two miles out of Nome, the Teller Road heads towards two peaks: Anvil Mountain to the left and Newton Peak to the right. Named for the anvil-shaped rock formation on the western side of the summit, Anvil Mountain is best known for the Cold War-era site on its eastern summit, part of a statewide communications system known by the code name "White Alice." The four giant, box-like antennas, which served to receive and transmit low-frequency microwave radio communications, were built to provide reliable communications to far-flung, isolated, and often rugged locales and to connect remote Air Force facilities with command centers in Alaska. The DEW Line—or Distant Early Warning Line—became obsolete with the advent of satellite communications in the 1970s and was deactivated.

One of four White Alice antennas on Anvil Mountain.

Access to dwarf alpine habitat on the summit of Anvil Mountain is possible by a gravel side road that originates from the Dexter Bypass Road (see Mile 2.8). The land is property of Sitnasuak Native Corporation, so please follow the posted rules. The top of the mountain affords sweeping views of the area and an assemblage of species not found at lower elevations. In spring the Kamchatka rhododendron and other dwarf tundra flowers produce a stunning carpet of color across the rocky surface. In most seasons, groups of muskox are found on the flanks or top of the mountain making this a reliable place to view bulls, cows, and calves at relatively close distances from the road. Birdlife includes species that favor lichen-covered rocks, dwarf prostrate willows,

The Kamchatka rhododendron grows on short stems close to the ground but the bloom is about two inches across.

American pipit

and other attributes of the alpine zone, such as American golden-plover, horned lark, northern wheatear, American pipit , red-throated pipit, and rock ptarmigan. Common raven build their nests on the antennas.

Reindeer from privately-owned herds are often close to town at fawning time in late April and May. Do not confuse these animals with caribou, which are state-managed wildlife and not known to be in these areas in the spring. Red fox are frequently seen scavenging on dead fawns. Grizzly and wolf are occasionally attracted to an easy meal at fawning time, especially at twilight.

▶ Mile 2.8: Dexter Bypass Road

Habitat: Dwarf tundra, side slopes

Open only in summer, the five-mile long Dexter Bypass Road links Teller Road and Kougarok Road and offers additional opportunities for muskox viewing. Access to Anvil Mountain is on the left, about a mile from the Teller Road. After passing the road summit, notice the horizontal lines running across the distant slope: the remnants

Dexter Bypass Road rises along the flank of Anvil Mountain.

of old ditch lines that carried water to mining operations and the bed of an old railroad line. The road ends at the intersection of Kougarok Road across from the small community of Dexter.

▶ Mile 3: Old Glacier Creek Road

This approximately five-mile, gravel, side loop passes through some popular blueberry picking spots and is often a good area to view muskox. The road overlooks the Anvil Creek mining area before joining up with the New Glacier Creek Road at Glacier Creek.

Raking ripe blueberries with a specially-made comb improves yields of picked berries.

▶ Mile 4.9: Anvil Creek

Teller Road crosses Anvil Creek one mile below the site of the 1898 gold discovery that triggered the Nome gold rush. From here you can view the wind turbines that form the start of Nome's efforts to harvest wind as an alternative energy source.

Harnessing the winds for energy.

▶ Mile 6: Turn-off to Glacier Creek Road

Glacier Creek Road runs approximately 30 miles up the east side of the Snake River. It becomes a rough four-wheel-drive road after it passes the Rock Creek Mine site three miles in and is not maintained in winter.

If you look north up the valley from Teller Road, you will see the pyramid-shaped peak of Mount Osborn on a clear day. At 4,714 feet, it's the tallest peak on the Seward Peninsula. The small lakes on either side of the road become ice-free earlier than large lakes in spring, offering waterbirds nesting areas close to coastal feeding areas. You may see tundra swan, Canada goose, American wigeon, northern shoveler, northern pintail, green-wing teal, greater and lesser scaup, red-breasted merganser, red-throated loon, Pacific loon, red-necked phalarope, glaucous gull, and mew gull. Rusty blackbird often appears in the shrubby edges of wet meadows in this area.

▶ Mile 7: Snake River Bridge

Habitat: River valley

The Snake River has a relatively short drainage that flows out of the south side of the Kigluaik Mountains. The bridge crossing is typical of the wide, vegetated valley with tall, dense willows growing along the banks of a narrow, swift-flowing river. The broad riparian habitat supports some of the highest densities of moose along the Nome road system.

Dog days on the Snake River.

The lower river moves lazily and boaters may put in at the bridge for a short day-long float trip downstream to take-out locations close to the airport or harbor.

The road is not maintained beyond the bridge in winter and is typically impassible due to deep snowdrifts. However, a walk, ski, or snowmachine ride along the

Snake River valley may reveal the tracks of moose, ptarmigan, red fox, snowshoe hare, mink, river otter, and beaver in the snow.

Northern harrier hunt for songbirds and small rodents where tundra meadows meet the hillside willows. Migrating sandhill crane pass overhead in May and September. Look for Arctic tern, cliff swallow, and tree swallow around the bridge and yellow warbler and Wilson's warbler in willow thickets nearby. Pink and chum salmon run upriver in late July and early August and coho salmon are found in the river from mid- to late August. Arctic grayling and Dolly Varden also are found in these waters.

Mile 7 to 36 Snake River to Feather River

Habitat: Dwarf tundra, human-modified, river valley

Cotton grass heads tossing in the wind.

Moving away from lowland tundra, the road crosses rolling hills, small creeks, and a major river and offers scenic views of tundra landscapes. Some road grades are steep and indicative of the deeply dissected short drainages characteristic of the southern Seward Peninsula. Each creek or river usually has a thin thread of dense vegetation that provides habitat, food, and refuge for mammal and bird species. The open tundra slopes have windswept waves of cotton grass showing their white blooming seed heads in early summer.

Muskox may be seen feeding on sedges, wildflowers, and berries on side slopes and ridgelines. Reindeer are sometimes present in small groups in tundra meadows or on side slopes, while moose frequent areas of sparse willows. Rough-legged hawk, gyrfalcon, and common raven nest and perch on rocky outcrops. Wilson's snipe is often heard in overhead display flights in May and June. Long-tailed jaeger, northern harrier, and short-eared owl are common when voles, lemmings, or small birds are abundant. Northern wheatear is often seen at the base of rocky slopes. Several species of warblers and sparrows prefer the tall willows along the road.

Fields of cotton grass may be seen in many areas along the road system.

▶ Sledge Island view

Seven miles off the coast, Sledge Island is visible on clear days from this section of Teller Road. Originally named Ayak, the island was home to about 50 Ayakmiut, who primarily hunted seals but also walrus when those animals migrated close to shore. The British explorer Captain James Cook landed on the island in 1778 and gave it an English name after a Native-made sled—or sledge—that he found there. The island's steep cliffs provide ledges, crevices, and burrows for nesting kittiwakes, murres, and puffins often seen along Nome's coast.

Sighting Sledge Island through the old timbers of an abandoned reindeer corral.

▶ Mile 11.3: Abandoned reindeer corral

On the left as you head north are remnants of an abandoned reindeer corral that was first constructed by the Bureau of Indian Affairs in the 1970s for a reindeer herding demonstration project. The local Sitnasuak Native Corporation took over the corral in the early 1980s and ran a herd of about 750 animals for several years. The corral fell into disuse after Sitnasuak got out of the business and distributed the reindeer to other herders.

▶ Mile 12.5: Penny River Bridge

Habitat: River valley, side slope

Below the bridge, the Penny River flows in braided channels through a narrow valley. During spring thaws, surging high waters and ice flows flood the valley and damage the tall willows that grow close to the river. But the resilient willows re-grow, making good browse for moose. Evidence of beaver feeding, cutting, and building dams and ponds is common in the drainage. Muskox may seek out the river or tall willows on hot summer days. River otter, though rarely seen, may be spotted in early winter eating coho salmon carcasses.

Looking upstream from Penny River Bridge.

The bridge crossing gives a good view of unusual birdlife and the passage of salmon as they return to spawn each year. Red-breasted merganser and harlequin duck like the swift-flowing water. Arctic tern, mew gull, glaucous gull, semipalmated plover, and spotted sandpiper are seen along the river.

Bank swallow excavate burrows in cut banks. American dipper, Arctic warbler, gray-cheeked thrush, and common and hoary redpoll are seen in this area. Pink, chum, and coho salmon; Arctic grayling; and Dolly Varden are found in the river.

▶ Mile 13.6: Possible raptor viewing

Habitat: Rock cliff, ponds

Driving north, the rocky outcrop on your right may host a nesting or perching site for rough-legged hawk, gyrfalcon, and common raven. Look to your left into the creek bottom to see an active beaver lodge with several dams and ponds.

▶ Mile 15: House/Cabin Rock

Habitat: Dwarf tundra

House Rock and Cabin Rock are local names for the obvious rock formation on the right. The Arctic ground squirrel, locally called "parky squirrel," is common on the dry, upper slopes of this hill. This location was once a popular squirrel trapping area when the skins were more in demand for clothing.

House Rock

As the road crests the hill, you are viewing the dramatic south face of the Kigluaik Mountain Range. Muskox often gather on these windblown summits and ridgetops in winter. Golden eagle, rough-legged hawk, gyrfalcon, and common raven perch or nest on rock outcrops and prominent high points. American golden-plover, northern wheatear, and American pipit frequent the area.

▶ Mile 19.4: Cripple River Bridge

Habitat: River valley, tundra meadow, human-modified

The steep road grade on either side of Cripple River gives a good overview of the thin thread-like river that runs through the valley. Gold mining activities occurred in the upper tributaries, as evidenced by the road and horizontal ditch lines, which are still visible on the upstream slopes and continue to trap water and snow.

The extra moisture encourages growth of taller shrubs and provides a small windbreak, attracting wildlife. An access road towards the coast begins near the bridge crossing private land. Look for harlequin ducks paddling swift river currents in late August or September. Pink salmon reach their upper spawning limit in the Cripple River. Dolly Varden fingerlings and spawning adults are food for river otters.

Pink salmon heading upstream to spawn.

▶ Mile 21: Turn-off

Habitat: Dwarf tundra, tundra meadow, human-modified

Heading north, a turn-off to a gravel pit on the right also offers off-road parking and access to tundra ridge hiking with great views of the surrounding area.

Not all milepost markers are in good condition and some are even missing. Set your odometer at the start of each road to pace yourself.

▶ Mile 26: Sinuk River Bridge

Habitat: River valley, side slope

The Sinuk River is the largest river crossing on the Teller Road, and the magnitude of the valley, river channels, craggy mountains, and rolling tundra—all in one panoramic vista—is an impressive sight. Meanwhile, the river channels shifting from year to year make this place a window on the ever-changing aspects of river systems.

Looking downstream from Sinuk River Bridge.

The bridge is a reliable spot to see salmon on their return upriver. Sockeye salmon travel 16 miles upriver to spawn in Glacial Lake in the heart of the Kigluaik Mountains. Chum, pink, and coho salmon reach their upper spawning limit about two miles above the bridge. Chinook salmon rarely travel as far as the bridge.

Birdlife tends to be those species attracted to flowing water and gravel bars, islands, and thick vegetation clustered in some sections of the river. Boating is possible in the early season when water levels are high but becomes questionable as summer progresses.

▶ Mile 29: View of the Kigluaik Mountains

Habitat: Tussock tundra, rocky slopes

The crest of the hill north of the Sinuk River offers a spectacular view of the Kigluaik Mountains on a clear day. Grizzly bear den in these rugged, remote mountains, and river drainages provide refuge for moose.

▶ Mile 31.7: Permafrost viewing

Just south of Livingston Creek, the tundra next to the road has sloughed away and exposed the permafrost beneath the surface layer of tundra plants and soil.

▶ Mile 34: Turn-off

Habitat: Tussock tundra, rocky slopes

A turn-off on your right heading north provides off-road parking and access to tundra ridge hiking with views of the mountains.

▶ Mile 36: Feather River Bridge

Habitat: River valley, dwarf tundra

The Feather River is a noisy, rocky, boulder-strewn river with a steep gradient, fast flow, and little vegetation. The landscape seems more barren, probably resulting from the impact of constant wind, long winters, and poor soil. Muskox and reindeer may be seen here, but other wildlife sightings are less frequent in this drainage. Arctic grayling are found in these waters and pink salmon in peak years.

Downstream from the bridge is an old road construction camp, gravel mine, and airstrip where the first of two transports of muskox from Nunivak Island took place in 1970. The herds have since established themselves throughout the peninsula.

In 1970, muskox packed in stout wooden boxes await release and a new life on the Seward Peninsula.

Mile 36 to 47 — Feather River to Tisuk River

Habitat: Tundra meadow, dwarf tundra

As the Teller Road skirts the western edge of the Kigluaik Range, it crosses higher and drier ground where plants and wildlife associated with dwarf tundra are found. The formidable mountain on the right has long been called Singatuk (also spelled Singatook) by the local Inupiat but others refer to it as 38-70, after its elevation (3,870 feet). Because of its height and isolation from other tall peaks, it is considered a "weather maker"—a place where clouds and precipitation gather. The King Islanders, who have a summer

Clouds gather around the base of Singatuk.

camp nearby, talk of wolverine in the area though the chances of seeing one are extremely rare. Teller herders graze their reindeer in open range, secure in the knowledge that caribou from the Western Arctic herd—perhaps discouraged by the Kigluaik Mountains to the north and east—seldom migrate here. Along with reindeer, muskox is the most common large mammal found along this section of road.

Rock ptarmigan prefer upper rocky slopes, and horned lark are most often seen in drier, open meadows. The lark's "horns" are small dark feathers above the eye. American pipit, northern wheatear, and red knot nest on high, dry ridges in this area.

Horned lark

King Island views

The next several miles of road offer views of King Island in clear weather. The island is ideally situated for harvesting the many seals and walruses that pass through the Bering Strait. Native people use the meat and blubber of seals and

Forty miles off shore is the ancestral home of the King Islanders.

walrus for food, the oil for cooking and heating, and carve the ivory into household and hunting implements. They would once split and dry the skins for use in construction of their homes and essential umiaqs, large open boats made from skins stretched over a wooden frame.

They also traded walrus skins to other mainland villages for the hides of caribou and furbearers. The King Islanders have long maintained a summer camp at Woolley Lagoon, where they continue to catch and dry salmon and gather greens and berries.

According to Inupiat legend, a huge fish caught up the Kuzitrin River was towed out to sea where it became King Island. Originally called Ukivok, the island once harbored a village of approximately 200 people. Captain Cook gave the island its present name after his lieutenant, James

A young hunter poses by an overturned umiaq, a skin-covered open wood frame boat used for hunting and travel.

King. In the early 1960s, when the Bureau of Indian Affairs closed the school, the island residents relocated to Nome, where they maintain a distinct cultural identity to this day. Some still voyage to the island to hunt in spring and pick greens in summer, keeping alive the dream of one day returning to their ancestral home.

▶ Mile 40: Side road to Woolley Lagoon

Habitat types: Dwarf tundra, tundra meadow, ponds

Winter trail markers lead the way to Woolley Lagoon.

This 100-foot-wide road is a public right-of-way that traverses lands privately owned by the King Island Native Corporation. It runs eight miles to traditional summer fishing camps at Woolley Lagoon. Please stay within 50 feet of either side of the road, and do not travel close to the lagoon or summer camps. The King Islanders value their privacy and request that you do not photograph their campsites.

As you turn onto Woolley Lagoon Road, a small pull-off immediately to your right is where King Islanders and many others driving the Teller Road collect drinking water. Some believe this very clear stream holds healing powers. A unique limestone outcrop, called Moon Mountains, is visible down the coast from Cape Woolley and is a wintering spot for muskox. Several rare plants have been identified in its unique micro-habitat.

Red fox feed on ground-nesting birds and abundant small rodents. Black-bellied plover nest near the end of the road. Semipalmated plover, Pacific golden-plover, semipalmated sandpiper, and western sandpiper are often seen on river gravel bars. Pomarine, parasitic, and long-tailed jaeger are also found here.

A moonscape at Moon Mountains with Sledge Island in the distance.

▶ Mile 46.5: View of raptor nest

Habitat: Rocky outcrop

As you approach the Tisuk River, scan downstream and across the river for a large nest of sticks on an orange lichen-covered rock outcrop. Built by golden eagles, it may be used by gyrfalcon when not occupied by eagles.

▶ Mile 47: Tisuk River

Habitat: River valley, side slope

The Tisuk River valley near the bridge is subject to huge ice build-ups that extend over the gravel bars and riverbanks and are slow to melt in the spring. Because of the ice, this area is poor fish habitat and willow growth is sparse along the riverbanks.

Due to gravel bars and winter ice build-up, plants fight for a toehold along the Tisuk River.

Mile 47 to 58 | Tisuk River to Bluestone River

Habitat: Tundra meadow, side slope, river valley

Mushrooms and dwarf birch glow in autumn's golden light.

The views of the Kigluaik Mountains recede as you travel across high, rolling hills of tundra meadows with occasional creek and river crossings. You may spot moose, grizzly, muskox, and reindeer on the surrounding slopes.

Note: You are entering "gold country" where much of the land is privately-held, and recreational gold panning is not allowed. Check with the Bureau of Land Management in Nome for information about land ownership and public use.

▶ Mile 52.7: Gold Run Creek

Habitat: River valley

The road parallels a somewhat narrow creek valley, making it easy to see water and shorebirds associated with flowing water as well as the wide variety of song-birds, such as thrushes, warblers, and sparrows that hang out in dense shrubs clustered at creek's edge. Arctic grayling, and some-times pink salmon, are found here.

Fox sparrow

▶ **Mile 53.7: Gold dredge**

Miners worked this dredge up and down the Bluestone River and Gold Run Creek in the early 1900s. Now it serves as a nesting and perching site for common raven.

▶ **Mile 54.9: Sullivan City**

Once a bustling mining camp and supply center, Sullivan City sprang up downriver from the dredge. Several small-scale mining operations continue today. This is privately-owned property and trespassing is forbidden.

Marooned dredges are remnants of the gold fever that once gripped this land.

▶ **Mile 56.9: Bluestone River Bridge**

Habitat: River valley, side slope, rocky outcrop

The Bluestone River is unlike other river crossings along the Teller Road because it flows northward to Imuruk Basin rather than south to Norton Sound. The river is deeply incised as it cuts through steep mountains, creating steep, rocky slopes and cliffs. The scenery is dramatic if you take time to climb to nearby hilltops.

The bridge is adjacent to a dome-shaped, rock cliff that has the color, vegetation, and appearance typical of the area. Rough-legged hawk, golden eagle, gyrfalcon, and common raven may nest on nearby rock cliffs. Say's phoebe sometimes nest under the bridge or on nearby cliff-side ledges or crevices. Northern shrike nest in tall willows along the river, and their predatory

Say's phoebe

diet includes small mammals and the young of other songbirds. Bluethroat nest in side drainages with mixed-height willows. Arctic grayling, and sometimes pink salmon, are present in the river.

Muskox tracks in the mud.

Mile 58 to 71 — Bluestone River to Teller

Habitat: Tundra meadow, side slope, dwarf tundra

High rolling tundra meadows punctuated with large flat-topped mesa-like hills extend for the next 10 miles, with an occasional glimpse of the north face of the Kigluaik Mountains in the distance. In some years, salmonberries are abundant across these high tundra meadows. In August you are likely to see whole families picking bucketfuls of the red- and peach-colored

Fireweed in full bloom in the meadows above Teller.

fruit here. As the road begins to descend to Grantley Harbor, enjoy sweeping views of Teller and the Teller sand spit. The village of Brevig Mission is visible on a clear day across the bay on the north shore of Port Clarence. You may see reindeer—owned by a Teller herder—and muskox grazing in the area. Common raven and glaucous gull feed on ripe salmonberries in late summer. American golden-plover, snow bunting, northern wheatear, and horned lark are found on rocky domes rising above the meadows.

Note: At mile 71, just before the road reaches the beach, a side road heads east into a housing complex built for Teller's growing population. Please respect residents' privacy and remain on the main road unless invited to visit. In Teller, please remain on the main roads and ask permission before taking photographs.

▶ Mile 72: Teller and Grantley Harbor

Habitat: Human-modified, coastal beach, tundra meadow, pond

Coming into Teller with Brevig Mission in the distance across the bay.

At Teller the road returns to sea-level where the environment is dominated by marine waters. Lowland meadows flank the coastline and a sandspit arcs away from the landmass in relatively shallow waters. Marine mammals, seabirds, and other new species are common sightings, allowing travelers to expand the list of wildlife found along

White wagtail

72 miles of mainland tundra. Look for spotted seals on calm days, their heads popping up inquisitively at the tip of the spit. Pelagic cormorant, pigeon guillemot, horned puffin, common eider, and black scoters are seen here. Some years, white wagtails nest in the local cemetery. Ask locally for directions and permission to view them.

The cycle of subsistence in Teller

Most Teller residents participate in some form of subsistence harvesting. In spring people eat fresh new willow shoots (called **sura** in Inupiaq) with seal oil. They gather sourdock, wild celery (called **tukaayuk**), and other local greens in summer. In late summer, they pick salmonberries and blueberries, and later crowberries. The root of a sweetpea (called **masru**) gathered in fall is prized. Some still hunt for "mouse nuts"—cottongrass seeds cached in grass tunnels by voles. Inupiaq tradition requires that you replace the seeds with some other bit of food.

Beach greens are tasty and nutritious too. They are high in vitamin C.

In the spring after the ice goes out and again in the fall, people use gillnets to catch herring, whitefish, and tomcod. In midsummer fish nets may be set perpendicular to shore. Wooden racks are hung with drying salmon along the beach and next to homes. Many people also have fish camps upriver or along the coast. All five salmon species swim through here, but the primary catch is red salmon, which migrate inland to spawning grounds at Salmon Lake. Chum salmon pass through in July bound for the Pilgrim River, while a second run arrives in

late August headed to spawning grounds in the Agiapuk River. Occasionally, a prized Chinook salmon turns up in a net. In September residents catch starry flounder in gillnets. In summer they fish upriver for northern pike using gillnets and fishing poles. In winter they catch pike with hand-lines from holes cut in the river ice.

Fishing is a way of life in coastal villages of Alaska, like Teller.

While freezers are stocked with moose and muskox, villagers also hunt seals—primarily spotted, ringed, and bearded seal. Seal meat and seal oil are staples in a traditional Native diet. How one learns to hunt, who one hunts with, how meat is divided and shared, how it is preserved, and the occasions where it is served continue to be the cultural glue that binds together a community like Teller.

A brief history of Teller

Before non-Natives settled in this region, there were no permanent settlements. People instead moved among small seasonal camps, following the fish and wildlife.

Drying racks haven't changed much in a century or more.

In 1848 the first commercial whaling ship sailed through the Bering Strait, followed soon after by traders. A Western Union expedition scouting a route for an intercontinental telegraph line across the Bering Strait spent the winter of 1866-67 camped on the spit across from Teller. From 1892 to 1900, the United States government operated a reindeer station nearby, named for United States Senator and Secretary of the Interior, Henry Moore Teller.

The town of Teller boomed in its current location in the early 1900s with the discovery of gold in the nearby Bluestone River and the passage of ocean vessels and barges traveling to the Kougarok gold fields farther inland. Teller also became a trading center for Inupiat from Diomede, Wales, Mary's Igloo, King Island, and the Russian coast. Many first relocated to Teller to take advantage of the economic opportunities and later to allow their children to attend school. During the early boom years, the town reached a population of about 5,000.

The worldwide flu epidemic swept through Teller in 1918. Two years later, an epidemic of tuberculosis decimated the Inupiat population. Many orphaned children were sent upriver to a Catholic orphanage at Pilgrim Hot Springs. Despite this devastating blow, the people and the community persevered.

Teller briefly drew international attention in May 1926, when Roald Amundsen and a crew of fifteen made the historic

An incongruous sight in tiny Teller.

first flight from Europe to North America in the airship Norge. They left from Spitsbergen, Norway, passed over the North Pole, and were forced to land at Teller due to weather, even though their destination was Nome.

Local residents' reliance on the area's many subsistence resources helped them weather the rise and fall of the mining and reindeer industries, the turbulent years of World War II when village men fought overseas, and the rapid changes that accompanied the influx of Western culture.

Today, Teller is an Inupiat village that blends a cash economy with subsistence hunting, fishing, and gathering. The primary employers include the school, city offices, Native corporations,

Caribou antlers decorate a Teller home.

a health clinic, power and water plants, and seasonal construction work. One locally-owned reindeer herd remains active, and some residents earn money selling ivory, antler, and bone carvings. Though casual observers may not see many subsistence activities underway, a peek in most residents' freezers reveals a host of wild foods that were harvested locally and delicacies acquired in trade from villages around the region.

Teller Fish and Meat is a processing plant in town.

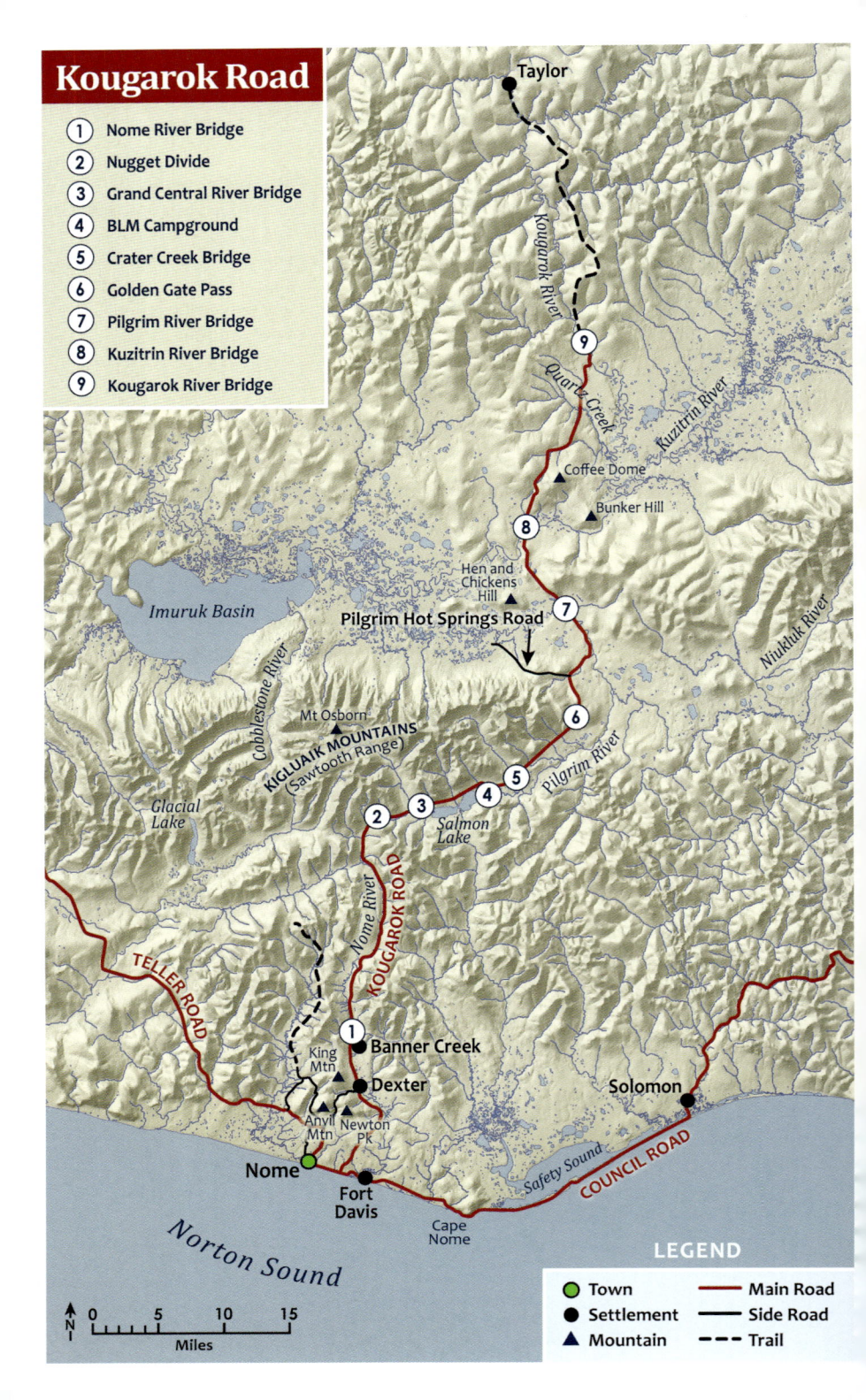

Kougarok Road

1. Nome River Bridge
2. Nugget Divide
3. Grand Central River Bridge
4. BLM Campground
5. Crater Creek Bridge
6. Golden Gate Pass
7. Pilgrim River Bridge
8. Kuzitrin River Bridge
9. Kougarok River Bridge

Taylor

Kougarok River

Quartz Creek

Kuzitrin River

Coffee Dome

Bunker Hill

Hen and Chickens Hill

Pilgrim Hot Springs Road

Niukluk River

Imuruk Basin

Cobblestone River

Mt Osborn

KIGLUAIK MOUNTAINS
(Sawtooth Range)

Pilgrim River

Glacial Lake

Salmon Lake

Nome River

KOUGAROK ROAD

TELLER ROAD

Banner Creek

King Mtn

Dexter

Anvil Mtn

Newton Pk

Solomon

Nome

Fort Davis

Cape Nome

Safety Sound

COUNCIL ROAD

Norton Sound

LEGEND

● Town	— Main Road
● Settlement	— Side Road
▲ Mountain	- - - Trail

N

0   5   10   15
Miles

Kougarok Road

A red fox in the autumn tundra pounces on its prey.

The official name is the Nome-Taylor Highway but local residents call this scenic well-maintained gravel road: the Kougarok Road. That's because the road ends at the Kougarok River Bridge, about 25 miles shy of Taylor. From here on it becomes a rough trail passable only by foot or All Terrain Vehicle (ATV). Don't be fooled by maps that show the road continuing on to Taylor.

The Kougarok Road begins at the edge of the Bering Sea, 1.6 miles east of Nome, and heads north for approximately 86 miles. Bisecting the spectacular Kigluaik Range, it crosses clear flowing streams that offer views up glacially-carved valleys. Past Salmon Lake, the terminus of the northernmost sockeye salmon run, the road moves into the rolling lowlands of the central Seward Peninsula. Birders often make this journey in search of the elusive bristle-thighed curlew and brightly-colored bluethroat.

Much of the highway parallels the route of an old railroad bed. In the early 1900s, the Seward Peninsula Railroad hauled passengers and freight from Nome to the gold fields in the interior. The railroad saw use into the late 1950s until construction of the highway in 1960 opened the region to automobiles. You can still spot trestles and tracks, although some of the tracks were sold to Disneyland in the early 1960s.

NOTE: The road to Pilgrim Hot Springs crosses private property owned by Bering Straits Native Corporation (BSNC) and Mary's Igloo Native Corporation. At the time of book printing, the roadway does not have a legal easement for public access. Visitors should check with land owners for access status and restrictions before attempting to cross private property. To obtain a permit to visit the Pilgrim Hot Springs orphanage and surrounding property, contact the BSNC office on Front Street, the Nome Visitor's Center, or the Aurora Inn.

Habitat: River valley, side slope, human-modified, rocky outcrop

This section of the Kougarok Road follows the Nome River Valley as it changes from a coastal zone of broad lowland meadow and open tundra to a narrow valley where the Nome River flows swiftly out of the Kigluaik Mountains. Paralleling the road is evidence of mining

The Nome River Valley

ditches that provided water for hydraulic mining of the gold-bearing layers of gravel at lower elevations. Shortly after leaving the coast, the road rises in elevation to cross old beach fronts from eons earlier when ocean levels were higher, or land levels lower. Thereafter, the road parallels the Nome River, sometimes next to riffles of water and sometimes on a distant side slope displaying the breadth and depth of the valley. Wildlife includes chance encounters of moose, muskox, and grizzly bear; good opportunities to see furbearers like beaver, fox, and river otter; and a wide variety and abundance of birds associated with rivers, ponds, shrubs, and meadow habitats. Reindeer herding is a local industry that has remained active since it began in the late 1800s. Many facilities used by herders can be seen along the road.

▶ Mile 0 to 5: Coastal lowlands

Habitat: Pond, tundra meadow

Spring provides some of the best opportunities to see semi-domestic reindeer along this section of road. Herders often move the animals closer to town during the April-May fawning season to protect the young from predation by wolves and grizzlies. Frequently heard in spring is the winnowing sound of Wilson's snipe made in flight by air rushing through its tail feathers. In summer the drive provides good bird watching for waterfowl, gulls, terns, and tundra species. Look in ponds for red-necked phalarope, northern pintail, wigeon, greater scaup, and Arctic tern. Long-tailed jaeger, Canada and cackling goose, sandhill crane, short-eared owl, bar-tailed godwit, whimbrel, and Wilson's snipe are found in tundra meadows.

American wigeon (male)

▶ Mile 3: The Nome landfill

The landfill draws many scavengers. Common raven is abundant year round. Glaucous, glaucous-winged, herring, mew, and—occasionally in summer—slaty-backed gulls show up as well. Red fox is also a frequent visitor to the facility.

In courtship, raven pairs fly together with wingtips almost touching and repeatedly dive and tumble in flight.

Mile 5 to 13 Nome River to Banner Creek

Habitat: River valley, side slope, human-modified

Female salmon lay their eggs in river gravels to be fertilized by the males.

Heavy mining activity along the lower stretch of the Nome River between 1900 and 1930 wiped out much of the fish and wildlife along the river, but life has since returned. Ponds and sloughs in the Nome River Valley provide important rearing habitat for juvenile coho salmon. Common raven and gulls feed on the carcasses of the adult salmon that return to spawn in August. Salmon often spawn near areas where spring-waters percolate through the gravel riverbed. The constant year-round flow prevents freezing and supplies oxygen to the developing eggs.

Dense willows on side slopes and tall willows along the river's edge harbor a mix of song birds, including gray-cheeked thrush, fox sparrow, yellow warbler, Wilson's warbler, Arctic warbler, and blackpoll warbler. The more open shrublands and tundra are home to orange-crowned warbler; yellow wagtail; savannah, white-crowned, American tree, and golden-crowned sparrows; Lapland longspur; and redpolls. Closer to the river and open water, semipalmated plover, wandering tattler, ruddy turnstone, spotted sandpiper, and gulls are found on gravel bars feeding at the water's edge.

Ptarmigan flock to feed on willow buds in winter.

Harlequin duck and red-breasted merganser coast along in the faster currents. Family groups of willow ptarmigan may be found in the river bottoms in summer. In the fall and winter, ptarmigan gather by the hundreds to feed on willow buds. Northern shrike will perch on the tallest willow branches to watch for a vole, a shrew, a young bird, or a large insect. Common raven sometimes nest on cabin roofs and ledges in the area. Groupings of species by habitat repeat themselves over and over again as the road passes through the same type of habitat at different locations.

Moose typically give birth in river valleys where the dense vegetation helps them be secretive and protective of their calves. Grizzlies are drawn to the calves. Beavers, and less abundant river otters, are active. In all seasons look for tracks and slides made by otters along the river-

Gangly young moose gather streamside.

bank, most obvious in snow. Muskox may be seen on side slopes or by the river. Coho salmon arrive here in August.

The spruce trees around cabins were transplanted from the boreal forest near Council. Due to climate warming, however, they are increasingly taking hold naturally in the lower valley.

▶ Mile 8.6: Community of Dexter

Heading north, the Dexter Bypass branches off on the left. The road offers a scenic return to Nome in summer and the possibility of seeing muskox. On the right are seasonal camps and year-round homes that make up the community of Dexter. The local watering hole, the Dexter Roadhouse, is often open late during the summer. Despite persistent rumors, the Dexter Roadhouse was not owned by Wyatt Earp. Instead, Earp ran the Dexter Saloon on Nome's Front Street.

Fall colors light up the flanks of Anvil Mountain along Dexter Bypass.

▶ Mile 9: King Mountain

King Mountain is the next hillside on the west side of the valley where it is easy to see the multiple cuts across its slopes for much of the year. Most cuts are man-made ditches that once brought water to Nome's gold fields for hydraulic mining operations. However, one cut is the old railbed of the Seward Peninsula Railroad, a narrow-gauge track used to transport people and equipment to the Kougarok gold fields. The line ended at the Kuzitrin River with a spur to Bunker Hill farther upriver. The railroad remained in operation into the mid-1900s.

▶ Mile 12.7: Reindeer corral

Reindeer round-ups are held at the corral once or twice a year. The animals are counted, inoculated, castrated, and ear-tagged. Bulls with prime antlers have their soft antlers removed for market in June. Up and down the Nome River Valley you may see groups of reindeer as herders move them toward the corral or north to their summer feeding grounds after the round-up.

▶ Mile 12.7: Railroad trestle and roundabout

Farther up the slope from the corral are the remnants of an old railroad trestle. The roundabout—a large circular platform where the last segment of rail would pivot 180 degrees to point the engine back toward town—is fast disappearing beneath the willows. Railroad construction began in Nome the summer of 1900. By 1906 the track stretched 80 miles to the Kuzitrin River. Like many other residents, the world famous musher Leonhard Seppala ran his dog team along the tracks using a small railroad car, called a "pupmobile."

The remnants of railroad tracks that once carried miners and equipment to the gold fields dot the valley landscape.

Besides servicing gold operations in the Kougarok Mining District, the railway opened land up to local residents for sightseeing, hunting, and fishing, much as the road does today.

▶ Mile 12.8: Community of Banner Creek

Heading north, the turn-off toward the river leads to the seasonal camps and year-round homes that comprise the community of Banner Creek. Just a short ways in is a gravel pit pond that may contain local nesting waterfowl, mew gull, Bonaparte's gull, and semipalmated plover. The edges with the tallest willows are

a good place to find blackpoll warbler. A large beaver lodge on the banks has helped to fertilize this once sterile gravel pit, which now supports juvenile coho salmon, Dolly Varden, and Arctic grayling.

Beaver are impressive builders. They construct their dams carrying mud and stones in their forearms and timbers in their teeth.

▶ Mile 13: Nome River Bridge near Banner Creek

Habitat: River valley, side slope

The Nome River is a good place to see salmon. Pink and chum salmon spawn in August, coho are usually present in August and September. Sockeye salmon, Arctic grayling, and Dolly Varden may be present. Look for Arctic terns fishing, harlequin duck and red-breasted merganser riding swift water, spotted sandpiper or wandering tattler at waterline, and northern shrike in the willowed river edges.

Siberian aster grow among the river rocks.

Mile 13 to 31.6 Upper Nome River Valley to Nugget Divide

Habitat: River valley, side slope, rocky outcrop

The elevation gradually increases as you continue up the Nome River Valley. Vegetation becomes less lush, hillsides steepen, and rocky outcrops and inland cliffs become more prominent. Low passes that cut through the mountains serve as natural migration corridors for animals moving about their home ranges.

Growing low on some side slopes are small stands of cottonwoods (formally called balsam poplar). This is an indication of thawed ground, which is often associated with ground water seepage or springs. Look for holes in the trees drilled by woodpeckers for their nests. Bluethroat have been spotted flitting through willows in the small side drainages, and common raven may nest in the branches of cottonwoods.

Be especially vigilant for raptors and their nests over the next 15 miles. Examine high rocky outcrops for splashes of their white excrement and rocks colored orange by lichen growing in the nutrient-rich areas beneath raptor nests and perch sites. Golden eagle build large stick nests that may be occupied later by falcons—birds that do not build nests from sticks. Rough-legged hawk soar high over the valley searching for Arctic ground squirrels and

An aerial view of a cliff-face raptor nest.

smaller rodents. Gyrfalcon cruise with strong wing beats low over the willow thickets attempting to surprise or flush ptarmigan or small birds. The squirrels often den in the loose gravel of the road shoulder.

▶ Mile 18: Cape Horn

Habitat: River valley, rocky outcrop

This high point in the road gives you an excellent view across the valley. Three ditch lines from earlier mining activities are apparent on the far side of the valley, especially where they cross the exposed rock face of Cape Horn. The ditches

originate near Hudson Creek about 12 miles upstream. Today these deep, wide gashes on the hillside offer cover and easier movement for wildlife—especially moose and grizzly bears. As Ditch Superintendent for the Pioneer Mining Company, Leonhard Seppala lived in the cabin, which featured a sauna and a dog barn for his team. A commemorative stone plaque, carved by Seppala himself, is on the

Ditch lines that carried water for hydraulic mining are etched into the exposed rock face of Cape Horn.

face of Cape Horn. Golden eagle, gyrfalcon, rough-legged hawk, and common raven alternately nest on or use the Cape Horn rock formation.

▶ Mile 25: Possible raptor viewing

Habitat: Rocky outcrop, side slope

As you head north, examine the rocky outcrops on your right for raptor nests. Bluethroat may be spotted flitting through the willows.

▶ Mile 26: Dorothy Creek

Habitat: Pond, river valley

As you continue north, Dorothy Creek flows out of mountains to the left past the red cabin on the far bank of the Nome River. About one mile up the creek is a scenic waterfall. While there is no trail, some people visit the waterfall by crossing the open tundra on the south side of Dorothy Creek and clambering down the steep incline either just above or below the waterfall.

American dipper may be seen flying through the waterfall to a dome-shaped nest made of moss on the rock face beyond. On the east side of the road, sockeye salmon use a series of man-made ponds as rearing habitat for juveniles. The pools were constructed during road renovations in 2004. Coho salmon also spawn in the vicinity.

American dipper

Mile 31.6 to 53.7 | Nugget Divide to Golden Gate Pass

Habitat: Dwarf tundra, side slope, rocky outcrop, medium tundra

The pass at Nugget Divide separates the Nome River watershed from the Pilgrim River watershed to the north. A Game Management Unit sign at this location marks the boundary between two drainage-based hunting areas, each with their own regulations. From here the road descends to the Grand Central River, a major tributary of the Pilgrim River (originally called the Kruzgamepa or Kutskumipa) then across Broad Pass to the intersection with the Pilgrim River Hot Springs Road.

▶ Mile 31.6–35.3: GMU sign to Grand Central River Bridge

Habitat: Dwarf tundra

This portion of the road is higher in elevation, better drained, and much drier than in lowland areas. The loose, dry soils are good for burrowing by ground squirrels, which are food for bears, wolves, and eagles. Golden eagle and rough-legged hawk nest in some of the rockier valleys. Snow bunting nest in natural rock cavities on high, barren slopes. Look for bird species that frequent alpine habitat, such as rock ptarmigan, American golden-plover, surfbird, horned lark, American pipit, northern wheatear, and Lapland longspur.

▶ Mile 35.3: **Grand Central River Bridge**

Habitat: River valley, side slopes, dwarf tundra

Grand Central Valley reaches deep into the Kigluaik Mountains. Heading north, the base of Mt. Osborn (at 4,714 feet, it's the Seward Peninsula's tallest peak) is visible far up the valley to the left. These mountains have classic U-shaped valleys carved by glaciers, but the ice has long since melted leaving only small lakes at the headwaters of the side drainages. Sockeye salmon migrate up Pilgrim River to Salmon Lake between late July and mid-August, and some continue up the Grand Central River as far as the bridge. Spawning occurs earlier at the

Grand Central River boasts a magnificent view up a glacially-carved valley.

bridge than Salmon Lake because the eggs develop more slowly in the cooler river temperatures than in the slightly warmer lake.

A grizzly bear checks the river for fish.

Grizzlies are fairly common around Grand Central and Salmon Lake valleys, especially in the late summer when spawned-out salmon and ripe berries are abundant. Harlequin duck and red-breasted merganser may be seen paddling in the fast waters, sometimes in the same place where the American dipper plunges into the water and walks on the river bottom searching for insect larvae.

Bluethroat, yellow warbler, Wilson's warbler, and Arctic warbler are relatively common species among the willows near the river and in small drainages along the road near the bridge. Arctic char entered the glacial lakes before the lakes long ago became landlocked and isolated from each other. Recent genetic testing shows that each lake's char has evolved into a distinct subspecies.

The rugged mountains close to the Grand Central River seem like natural habitat for Dall sheep, but you won't find them there. Biologists speculate that vegetation is too sparse on the rugged upper slopes and high alpine meadows where sheep prefer to feed in relative safety from predators. Recent finds of old sheep skulls, however, have ignited debate on whether wild sheep once populated the area.

The rugged Kigs seen from the air.

▶ Mile 36: **Spring-fed drinking water**

Just past the entrance to the Salmon Lake Lutheran Bible Camp, water from a nearby spring is piped to the side of road. Many residents stop here to fill their containers with cold, clear drinking water.

▶ Mile 39.9: **Salmon Lake Campground**

Habitat: Medium shrub

Salmon Lake is the only public campground on the Nome road system.

Heading north, an access road on your right leads to a lakeside campground that is maintained by the Bureau of Land Management. It has a sandy beach, picnic tables, barbeque pits, a trash bin, and a restroom that is open during snow-free months. There is no running water.

Bluethroat frequent the area. Red-necked grebe, red-throated loon, long-tailed duck, and red-breasted merganser populate the lake in summer. Midpoint along the banks of the lake is an abandoned village site.

The northern-most run of sockeye salmon return here to spawn in mid-August. Mew gulls and glaucous gulls come to feed on spawned-out salmon, as do red foxes and the occasional grizzly bear. The best time to see a bear is in the early morning or late evening. Look for their tracks in the sand.

Judging by its size, this track is probably from a cub of the same year.

History of salmon in Salmon Lake

Miners in the early 1900s reported the shores of Salmon Lake were red with spawned-out salmon and it seemed the fish were inexhaustible. But increased access to the lake—first by the Seward Peninsula Railroad along the south side of

the lake and later by the road—led to continued overharvest. With fewer decayed salmon carcasses supplying nutrients, the lake was no longer fertile enough to feed the young salmon fry. Decreasing salmon numbers in the 1960s resulted in increasingly lower catch limits for subsistence salmon fishing and in 1972, Salmon Lake was closed to salmon fishing during the spawning season.

If you plan to go fishing at Salmon Lake, first check with ADF&G for any fishing restrictions.

In 1997 the Norton Sound Economic Development Corporation, the Alaska Department of Fish and Game, and the Bureau of Land Management began working cooperatively to make more food available for young sockeye salmon by increasing the nutrient levels in Salmon Lake. By 2004 a record-breaking run of sockeye salmon had returned to the lake and, for the next several years, the runs provided additional fishing opportunities along the Pilgrim River. A severe downturn in returns at the end of the decade, however, resulted in new fishing restrictions and a renewed restoration effort.

Mile 40 to 53.6 Salmon Lake Campground to Pilgrim Hot Springs turn-off

Habitat: Side slope, rocky outcrop, dwarf tundra

Local residents call this area Broad Pass. Glaciers sculpted the land, forming ridges and rock piles (glacial moraines) as they advanced and leaving rocky rubble on the valley floor as they retreated. The shallow, rocky, and well-drained soils support dwarf tundra vegetation typically found at higher elevations.

Looking towards Pilgrim River valley from Broad Pass.

The winter winds blow fiercely through here and the tripods that mark the winter trail are placed close together to guide snow machines and dog teams through white-out conditions. Scan the large outcrops high on the slopes to your left for raptor nests. Look for birds that frequent ponds and alpine habitat.

Arctic ground squirrel, snowshoe hare, and red fox may be abundant in this area in some years. Muskox sometimes feed and rest on surrounding slopes.

▶ Mile 49: View of Iron Creek Bridge

Across the valley at the base of the far hills, you can still see the old train trestle spanning Iron Creek, just above its confluence with the Pilgrim River.

▶ Mile 50 to 53.6: Golden Gate Pass

Habitat: Side slope, dwarf tundra

Golden Gate Pass divides the gold-laden creeks and rivers to the south from Pilgrim and Kuzitrin Rivers, which are less rich sources of ore. To the east, a low, wide pass leads to the upper reaches of the Niukluk River, which flows southeast toward Council, White Mountain, and Norton Sound. This pass is a migration corridor into the Pilgrim River drainage for the Western Arctic caribou herd in years when they winter on the central Seward Peninsula. Domestic reindeer graze on open range land in summer.

American golden-plover, northern wheatear, American pipit, and Lapland longspur are common in the tundra areas.

Reindeer are often spotted along the road.

▶ Mile 53.6: Side trip to Pilgrim Hot Springs

Habitat: Dwarf tundra, rocky outcrop, side slope, tundra meadow

Note: At the bottom of Golden Gate Pass where the road makes a sweeping curve to the right, a marked turn-off to the left leads to Pilgrim Hot Springs. The road traverses private property and travelers must obtain permission to access beforehand. Look for contact information under Planning Your Visit (pg. 152).

Although this 7-mile side trip offers excellent vistas and access to a unique and historic setting, sections of the road are very rough and, if flooded, may be impassible. The road summit, 2.5 miles from the turn-off, offers a dramatic view of the north face of the Kigluaik Range and an expanse of wetlands in the lower Pilgrim River

Beware of wash-outs along the road to Pilgrim Hot Springs. Help is not readily available in this remote area.

Valley. The road traverses several distinctly different habitats on the way to the hot springs.

American golden-plover, snow bunting, horned lark, and northern wheatear are common in the dwarf tundra of the summit. Gyrfalcon and rough legged hawk find perches in rocky outcrops. Sandhill crane perform impressive courtship displays in late May or early June and congregate in tundra meadows before their fall migration. Whimbrel nest in the moist lowland tundra meadow. Look for tundra swan, American wigeon, and other ducks among the ponds and Wilson's, yellow, and Arctic warbler flitting through the surrounding shrubs.

Beaver lodges and dams may be active. Muskrats in the winter will create mounds of vegetation over a hole in the ice—called "push-ups"—when their numbers are high.

A warmer micro-habitat

Cottonwoods flourish and spring snows melt early at Pilgrim Hot Springs because of the warming influence of the local geothermal springs. The open water and grassy meadows provide a springtime oasis for waterfowl that sometime arrive when the surrounding landscape is still snowbound. You may find birds here that are not often seen elsewhere in the region.

Alder flycatcher, varied thrush, northern shrike, rusty blackbird, black-capped chickadee, solitary sandpiper, northern goshawk, and tree swallow frequent the area as well as Wilson's, yellow, and Arctic warbler. Cliff swallow nest under the eaves of several buildings.

A fertile oasis greets visitors to Pilgrim Hot Springs.

Pilgrim Hot Springs History

Originally a gold rush resort and later a Catholic mission, the site is listed on the National Register of Historic Places. The buildings are what remain of a Catholic orphanage and boarding school that operated at this location between 1918 and 1941 after a series of epidemics devastated most of the region's villages. The mission grew much of its own food in gardens that flourished in the warmed soils. Former students tell of the great trauma they suffered at having lost their families and communities, but they also remember the joys of living in this unique setting.

Several buildings remain from the old Catholic orphanage, including the church.

Pilgrim Hot Springs was purchased from the Catholic Bishop of Northern Alaska in 2009 by Unaatuq, LLC, a consortium of Native Corporations and non-profits in the Bering Straits region.

Mile 53.6 to 86 Golden Gate Pass to end of maintained road

Habitat: Dwarf tundra, rocky outcrop, river valley

Rounded mounds called pingos have an ice core.

After descending from the pass, the Kougarok Road crosses broad, flat river valleys with wide flood-plains that are unique to the interior portion of the Seward Peninsula. Rugged lowlands with poor drainage are cracked and buckled and marked by small hills, called pingos, and blocky patterns, called polygons. This type of land surface is called thermokarst and its features result from the melting of ground ice in a region underlain by permafrost.

The road bisects the Pilgrim River valley and crosses the Kuzitrin River valley before entering the interior uplands. The uplands are characterized by broad, rounded hills with sparse vegetation and deep, rounded valleys with vast expanses of tussock tundra habitat. The summer climate can be hot enough to generate thunderstorms and lightning strikes commonly set off tundra fires in the area, leading to hazy summer skies. Ash from the fires fertilizes the thin layer of soil and produces lush white areas of cotton grass when it blooms in late June.

▶ Mile 58: Possible raptor viewing

Habitat: Rocky outcrop, river valley

Use binoculars to scan the rock cliff directly across the river from a large subsistence camp for a pair of nesting rough-legged hawks.

▶ Mile 60.3: Pilgrim River Bridge

Habitat: River valley

Pilgrim River Bridge

The Pilgrim River crossing brings you close to groves of cottonwood that are abundant in this section of the valley. The presence of warmer soils associated with ground water springs contributes to the growth of deciduous trees. A lower understory of tall, dense willow and alder attracts birds that are similar to those found at Pilgrim Hot Springs and often associated with boreal habitats. In the flood zone near the bridge, numerous beaver dams block the side sloughs and create ponds that are used by a variety of water birds. Arctic tern and gulls perch on the bridge railing to rest between feeding flights above the river. The tall vegetation adjacent to the north side of the bridge is a reliable place to find blackpoll warbler and northern waterthrush.

Moose depend on the Pilgrim River for critical winter habitat. While moose typically disperse to willow-covered tributaries and side slopes in summer, cows and calves may remain along the main river in summer to feed on nutritious new shoots that spring from the ever-shifting gravel bars and shoreline.

Sockeye salmon and a few Chinook salmon pass under the bridge on their way to Salmon Lake to spawn in July and August. Chum, coho, and pink salmon spawn between the bridge and Pilgrim Hot Springs. Whitefish sometimes school in the area close to freeze-up. Burbot and northern pike are found in these waters.

Sockeye salmon

▶ Mile 61: Pilgrim River overlook

Habitat: Pond, tundra meadow, river valley

Beyond the Pilgrim River Bridge, the road continues uphill and offers sweeping views of a network of lakes and the meandering river valley. North of the Pilgrim River drainage is a large hill topped with a series of granite rock outcroppings known as Hen and Chickens because of its resemblance to a small flock at certain angles. A cross was placed at the summit in memory of a priest who died in a blizzard on his way to the orphanage.

Sandhill cranes cross the north face of the Kigluaik Mountains. Hen and Chickens is in the foreground.

Look for waterfowl species that typically frequent ponds and tundra meadows: tundra swan, Canada goose, red-necked grebe, and puddle ducks. Muskox sometimes feed in the grassy meadows at the base of Hen and Chickens in summer and spend the winter on the summit. Moose frequent the river valley.

▶ Mile 64 to 65: Swan Lake

Habitat: Pond, tundra meadow

Red-necked grebe nest on floating platforms.

The northernmost lake is called Swan Lake but several lakes in this area may hold a wide variety of birds. Tundra swan with cygnets, Canada goose, sandhill crane, northern shoveler, black scoter, long-tailed duck, greater and lesser scaup, and canvasback frequent the ponds. Red-necked grebe build floating nest platforms. The perimeter of meadow habitat with threads of water drainages are good places to find Pacific golden-plover. Look for signs of beaver and muskrat.

Mile 67.5: Kuzitrin River Bridge

Habitat: River valley, pond, human-modified

The Kuzitrin River Bridge had its origins in Fairbanks. It was originally named the Cushman Street Bridge when it was built across the Chena River in the heart of downtown Fairbanks in 1917. In the 1950s the bridge was replaced with a concrete span and the original metal bridge was disassembled, shipped down the Chena, Tanana, and Yukon rivers and barged up the Bering Sea coast to Nome. It was hauled in sections up the Nome-Taylor Highway and reassembled in its current location in 1958.

Just upriver from the bridge at the confluence with the Kougarok River are the remains of sod houses, a seasonal camp where local Inupiat caught and preserved broad whitefish. Some local people still seine or set nets through the ice for these fish, and huge runs may be visible from the bridge shortly before freeze-up in October. Northern pike and burbot also feed upon whitefish, as well as many gulls and common raven staying well into October. During the gold rush, the Seward Peninsula Railway ended upriver at Bunker Hill where an aerial tramway carried people and equipment across the river. A road at the end of the tram went on to Taylor and other gold mining areas, but the first half has since been reclaimed by the tundra. The remainder of the road is a rough ATV trail that heads north from the Kougarok bridge.

The bridge crossing is a good place to find multiple swallow species flying in the same area. Cliff swallow typically build gourd-shaped mud nests under the bridge, tree swallow nest in the nearby cottonwoods or nest boxes at camps, and bank swallow nest in mud cut banks along the river's edge. Look for Say's phoebe close to the small cabins near the bridge and rusty

The re-assembled bridge at Kuzitrin River was formerly known as the Cushman Street Bridge in Fairbanks.

blackbird, northern waterthrush, and blackpoll warbler in the tall vegetation that flanks the river. Moose depend on the Kuzitrin drainage for winter habitat.

▶ Mile 68.5: Ponds and pingos

Several small lakes and ponds sprinkle the landscape on either side of the road. Look for a small hillock just beyond the first lake. This lone pingo rises above the surrounding flat tundra meadow and serves as a convenient lookout for hunters such as foxes, wolves, hawks, owls, and jaegers. The soil on the tops of pingos is fertilized by predator feces and prey remains and generally supports lush and diverse vegetation. Arctic ground squirrel and fox sometimes dig dens in these mounds. With climate change, the expanse of permafrost is shrinking and with it, the number of pingos. Surf scoter nest at the ponds although the males return to the coast later in the season. Long-tailed duck and red-throated loon frequent the ponds while whimbrel may be seen in adjacent meadows.

Habitat: Side slopes, tundra meadow

You will notice many small active and abandoned mining operations in the creeks along this stretch of road. Please do not venture onto people's private property.

The road initially winds through side-slope shrubs of willow and alder. Ptarmigan and red fox are often seen here, as are hares and weasels in years of abundance. Vantage points offer opportunities to scan the valley and slopes for bears, moose, and muskox. Caribou migrating to the central and western Seward Peninsula in some winters may be found along this stretch of road. Wolf are more numerous and form larger packs than in areas to the south, but they are still wide-ranging, wary, and not easily seen.

Caribou begin their migration across snow packed mountains to reach their summer calving grounds.

Continuing north, you soon enter broad, rolling, moist tundra hills, home to voles and lemmings whose populations can fluctuate dramatically from year to year. In abundant years, look for the slender-bodied northern harrier flying low and the rough-legged hawk circling overhead in search of these small rodents. The numbers of short-eared owl and snowy owl rise and fall with the rodent population. Whimbrel and bar-tailed godwit nest in this habitat. Ptarmigan, red poll, and white crowned sparrow frequent the shrubby draws and perch on the willows that grow by the roadside where snow accumulation and runoff from the road provide additional moisture.

▶ Mile 72: Bristle-thighed curlew vicinity

Heading north, the sight of a large dark hill on the right—called Coffee Dome —signals to birders that they are in bristle-thighed curlew country. While the curlews nest in similar habitats elsewhere on the Seward Peninsula, this is one spot on the road system that is very close to their nesting grounds. Even so, it's an arduous 45-minute walk through ankle-twisting hummocks up the hillside to

Birders pick their way across uneven tundra to check the area around Coffee Dome for the prized bristle-thighed curlew.

the left, opposite Coffee Dome. If you are very lucky, or very patient, you may see the birds from the road as they fly between the hills. Curlews arrive in late May, sometimes before the road is open all the way, and may be present in this location into July. In mid to late August, you may spot them by the ponds near Nome as they prepare for their fall migration: a non-stop transoceanic flight to wintering grounds in southwestern Pacific Ocean islands.

For the best chance of seeing this large, tawny, long-billed shorebird, connect with a local guide or birding group or check with the Nome Visitor's Center.

▶ Mile 85: Quartz Creek airstrip

The Quartz Creek bush airstrip, up a short dirt road to the left, provides a jumping-off spot to mining claims at Serpentine Hot Springs and other points beyond the road system. It is also a staging area for ADF&G wildlife surveys. The airstrip was built during the road construction years and is still maintained by the state transportation department.

A number of cabins in this area attract Say's phoebe, American robin, and tree swallow.

The Quartz airstrip is often used to access the interior of the peninsula.

▶ Mile 86: Kougarok Bridge

Habitat: River valley, tundra meadow

Though built to accommodate the road from Bunker Hill to Taylor in the early 1900s, the bridge is as far as you can go by highway vehicle. From here a rough, unmarked, and sometimes impassable ATV trail leads to Taylor where family-owned mines still operate.

Canada goose frequent the river and nearby tundra habitat and the white-fronted goose is sometimes found on small ponds in this area. Bluethroat can be found on shrubby river banks. Arctic grayling are the most likely fish to be seen from the bridge.

A Canada goose has built its nest overlooking the river.

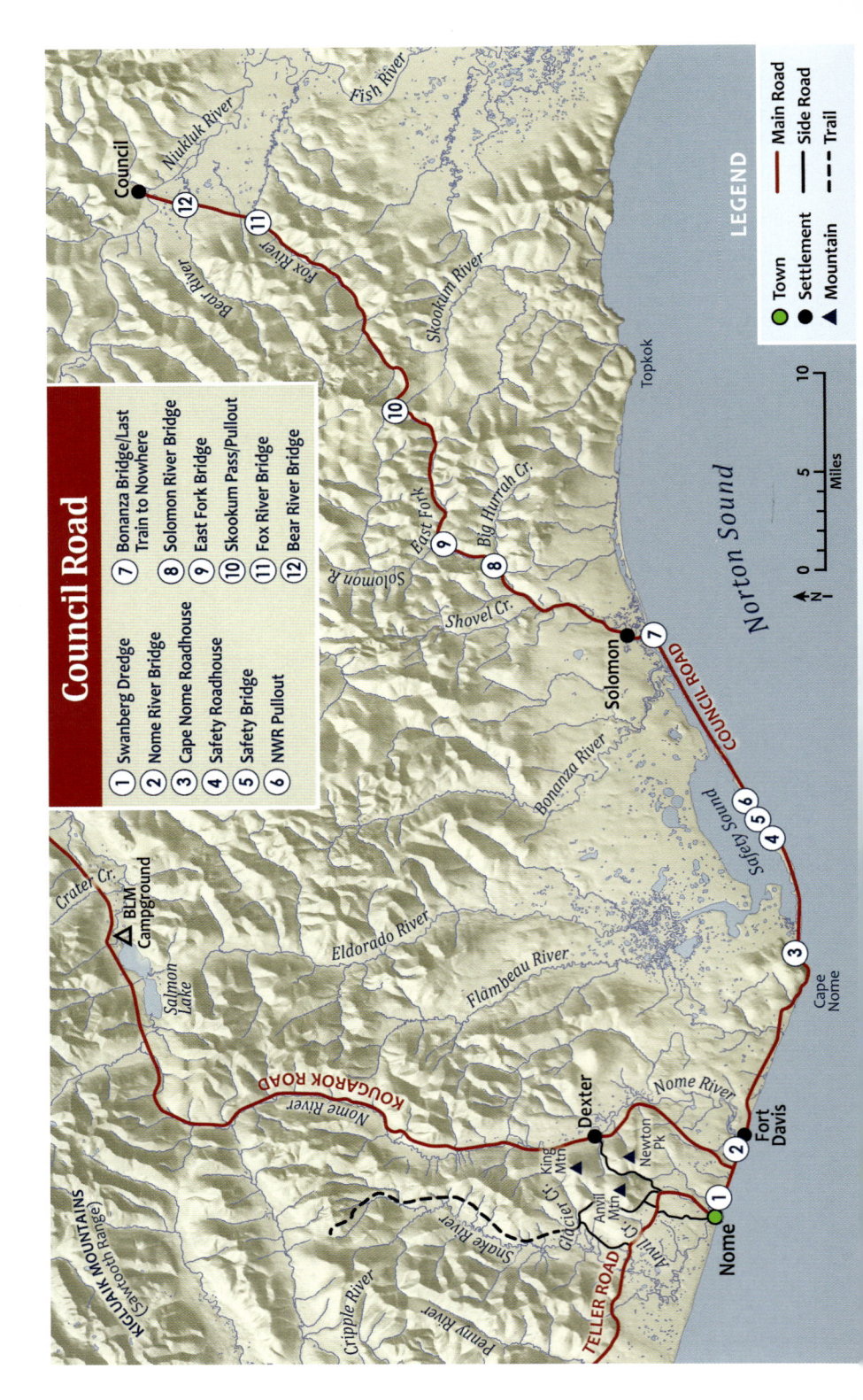

Council Road

① Swanberg Dredge	⑦ Bonanza Bridge/Last Train to Nowhere
② Nome River Bridge	⑧ Solomon River Bridge
③ Cape Nome Roadhouse	⑨ East Fork Bridge
④ Safety Roadhouse	⑩ Skookum Pass/Pullout
⑤ Safety Bridge	⑪ Fox River Bridge
⑥ NWR Pullout	⑫ Bear River Bridge

LEGEND

- Town
- Settlement
- Mountain
- Main Road
- Side Road
- Trail

Miles 0 5 10

N

Norton Sound

KIGLUAIK MOUNTAINS (Sawtooth Range)

Crater Cr.
BLM Campground
Salmon Lake
Eldorado River
Flambeau River
Cripple River
Penny River
Snake River
Glacier Cr.
Dry Cr.
Anvil Mtn
King Mtn
Newton Pk
Nome River
KOUGAROK ROAD
TELLER ROAD
Nome
Fort Davis
Dexter
Cape Nome
Safety Sound
COUNCIL ROAD
Solomon
Bonanza River
Shovel Cr.
Big Hurrah Cr.
East Fork
Solomon R.
Skookum River
Topkok
Fox River
Bear River
Niukluk River
Fish River
Council

Council Road

Sandhill cranes appear very dignified until they begin their lively mating dance, which starts with a deep bow followed by great leaps, hops, skips, turns, and more bows.

This 72-mile gravel road traverses every type of habitat along the Seward Peninsula road system from coastal beaches and wetlands, through tundra meadows and high dwarf tundra, to a river valley at the western edge of the boreal forest. The route also offers glimpses of the region's early 1900s gold rush, including "The Last Train to Nowhere" and the gold rush era town of Council on the Niukluk River. The wooden tripods that follow the coast mark the route of the Iditarod Trail and other winter trails.

River crossing: The seasonal community of Council is on the opposite bank of the river. It may be reached by boat or high-clearance 4WD vehicles in low water – only if you know the route. It may be possible to get a ride with a local resident or follow them across. Otherwise, do not attempt to cross.

Mile 0 to 4 | Nome to Nome River Bridge

Habitat: Coastal waters, beaches, human-modified

The seasonal coastline

The Bering Sea is always by your side for the first 33 miles of the Council Road. During long winter months when daylight is fleeting and average temperatures hover around 7°F, the coastline is encased in ice and snow but as days lengthen and the cold lifts, spring arrives in a hurry drawing life back into the landscape.

Shortly after the ice leaves, typically between late May and mid-June, young salmon and Dolly Varden fingerlings—no bigger than a pinkie—exit the rivers for the sea. Herring are the first to migrate up the coast from the Yukon River Delta followed closely by capelin, which often come to the beach on the evening of a high tide to spawn in the sand.

You can often figure out what species of fish are present by the birds that come to feed. Excited flocks of gulls and kittiwakes are drawn to schools of herring. Arctic terns—too small to grasp a robust 8-inch herring—will look instead for a slim 6-inch capelin, a smelt, or a 2-inch salmon fingerling that they can easily grip in their bill.

Pelagic cormorant

Several species of loons, which nest in nearby ponds, often fly over the road on their way to feed in coastal waters. Meanwhile, horned puffin, murres, and pelagic cormorant nest at distant rocky headlands, flying to and from nearshore and coastal feeding areas.

In late fall hundreds of beluga whale on their southward migration may be seen in close to the shoreline chasing schools of tomcod (saffron cod).

In winter shore-fast sea ice typically extends a long ways offshore. The shallow waters beneath this ice shelf are shaded and particularly salty, luring deep-water species such as king crab closer to shore. Local residents cut holes in the ice and drop in crab pots or hand-lines to catch this Bering Sea treat. Marine algae grow in these seemingly inhospitable conditions and attach to the underside of the ice. During spring melt, the algae drop into the water causing a plankton bloom, which feeds herring and other fish on their northward migration.

Slush ice forms on the sea at the beginning of freeze-up.

Beyond this zone, pack ice moves with the wind and currents, often opening a channel of water—called a lead—between the two types of ice. You may spot ringed, spotted, bearded, and occasionally ribbon seals either on the ice or in the water.

Spotted seals are often found within the outer margins of shifting ice floes.

Nome's "Golden Beaches"

Beginning in the summer of 1899, thousands of men, women, and children worked shoulder-to-shoulder to glean treasure from these shores after news of Nome's "Golden Beaches" rocketed around the world. To this day, hearty independent miners continue to work many area beaches with high bankers and sluice boxes. Most find themselves braving the cold waters in wetsuits to operate small, modern, floating suction dredges — essentially vacuuming ore-bearing materials off the ocean floor.

A modern dredge sucks ore-bearing materials off the ocean floor.

▶ Mile 0.5: East End Park ponds

Habitat: Ponds, tundra meadow

The city park at the east edge of Nome is a hidden gem of pond and tundra habitat. Birds flock here, especially during the early days of spring-thaw when the pond is an ice-free oasis amidst broad areas of frozen ocean. With the constant arrival and stopover of migrant waterbirds, this revolving door is worth checking frequently during late May and early June, and species associated with beach areas and marine waters are just steps away. At least 40 bird species, including waterfowl, shorebirds, raptors, gulls, terns, swallows, and songbirds (warblers and sparrows), can be seen at this location over time. Muskrat, red fox, mink, lemming, vole, and shrew are also common in meadows.

▶ Mile 1: Swanberg Dredge

Habitat: Ponds, tundra meadow, human-modified

Swanberg Dredge

This 1940s-era gold dredge is still afloat in its dredging pond but saw little action in its day. By the time the machine arrived, shipped in pieces from Seattle in 1946, World War II had ended and gold prices were falling. The dredge was repossessed by the bank in 1947 and never operated again. Interpretive signs tell the story and a boardwalk across the wetlands provides enhanced bird viewing. Common raven may nest on the dredge. Long-tailed duck, greater scaup, red-throated loon, green-winged teal, northern phalarope, and mew gull are regular species at the small dredge pond adjacent to the road.

▶ Mile 1.6: Intersection with Kougarok Road

The road junction is marked by ponds and tundra meadows within sight of the coastal beachline. Loons, red-breasted merganser, long-tailed duck, scoters,

gulls, and Arctic tern are common on the marine water and sometimes venture inland to ponds or tundra tussocks. Less frequently, Aleutian tern and long-tailed jaeger may be interspersed among perched glaucous and mew gulls near the road.

Red-throated loon and chick

▶ Mile 3.5: Nome River Bridge and estuary

Habitat: Estuary

The bridge marks a mixing zone where fresh river water meets tidal salt water and turns brackish. This creates a blend of water types and habitats and attracts many different birds to areas of open water or the mud-bar edges of islands. Birds forage, loaf, and roost—sometimes in tight clusters of mixed species—making this a good spot for lengthy observations. Wide meadows and broad, lazy bends in the river also attract geese, cranes, shorebirds, and gulls in good numbers, even unusual species like Arctic loon, red knot, black-tailed godwit, red-necked stint, ivory gull, and white wagtail. Starry flounder and marine sculpin are food sources that attract birds to the mud flats. From the bridge you may see chum and pink salmon in July and coho salmon in mid-August. Dolly Varden and burbot are also found in the Nome River.

Northern pintails (female) preening.

▶ Mile 3.7: Fort Davis

Beyond the bridge, a long line of small buildings hugs the coast where a U.S. Army post once stood during the early gold rush. Fort Davis was dismantled in 1923 as Nome's economy declined. The buildings you see today are locally-owned hunting and fishing subsistence camps. The Inupiat used this area well before the soldiers arrived because of diverse and abundant birds, fish, and mammals. Please do not disturb or trespass.

Mile 4 to 12 — Nome River to Cape Nome

Habitat: Tundra meadow, ponds

This section of road parallels the coast then moves inland across rolling tundra sliced by bands of thick shrubs and vegetation that grow along the banks of creeks tumbling down steep slopes. The tundra's small elevated ridges and grassy tussocks provide good nesting and perching places for birds, especially jaegers, gulls, snipe, whimbrel, and plovers. These species are common along this section of road but usually require a keen eye to detect. The open vegetated tundra provides nesting areas for willow ptarmigan, savannah sparrow, and Lapland longspur and nearby shrubby areas add gray-cheeked thrush, Wilson's warbler, and several sparrow species to the list of common birds. Short-eared owl and northern harrier may be seen hunting small mammal prey.

The east flank of Cape Nome looks out across lowland areas of vegetated tundra.

▶ Mile 9.4: Hastings Creek

Habitat: Estuary

The crossing offers expansive views of a variety of creek-side habitats, each with its own distinctive characteristics. In spring the upstream portion of the creek is filled with thick layers of glaciered ice that build up from winter's continual freezing of the spring waters that flow year-round into the creek. This late flow of melt water attracts waterbird species long after other areas are ice-free. Driftwood collects in the deeper pools around the road crossing, carried in by wind-driven storm tides. Beaver and river otter are likely to be found here and insects hatch in the racks of logs, attracting many birds. West of the bridge, on the elevated gravel pit that is a remnant of past road construction, the semipalmated plover often comes to pick at the exposed gravel. The surrounding steeper slopes

Bar-tailed godwit

are home to eastern yellow wagtail and bank swallow where the silty cap of soil above the gravel is exposed and used for nesting. The south edge of the gravel pit overlooks the lower portion of the creek—a relatively wide, braided delta where it exits to Norton Sound—and the mix of waterfowl, shorebirds, gulls, terns, and songbirds is constantly changing as summer advances. This is one location where an unusual species, the stilt sandpiper, has been seen more than once.

Mile 12 to 14 · Cape Nome

Habitat: Side slope, rocky outcrop, coastal water, human-modified

The road returns ocean-side to hug the base of a prominent rocky headland called Cape Nome: a towering landmass of steep rocky slopes, an active rock quarry, and

Storm clouds gather over Cape Nome in the distance.

very narrow beach zones. Deep waters and upwelling currents make this a particularly active area for invertebrate marine life, which in turn attracts marine mammals, fishes, and birds in large numbers. Deep snow that collects on the Cape's steep slopes results in increased soil moisture and encourages dense alder and willow growth. Land animals seek refuge and secrecy in this unique combination of rocky slopes and thick vegetation.

Grizzly bears may bed down in the dense shrubs during the day, waiting to walk the beach at night in search of a dead seal, walrus, or whale that has washed ashore. Red fox, gulls, jaegers, and common raven also scavenge the beaches throughout the long summer days. Smaller mammals, such as fox, hare, and porcupine inhabit the slopes of Cape Nome and resident bird species flock to the abundant alders and willows for feeding and roosting. Moose may seek protection from adverse weather in the dense alders.

Thick alders on Cape Nome provide cover for birds and other animals.

Human history

Hunters have long found Cape Nome to be an ideal lookout for seals, whales, and walruses, and a prosperous village once existed on its lower slopes. Up to 100 people lived in the village of Ayasayuk, a choice spot not only for abundant marine life but close proximity to fishing, waterfowl, wild greens, and berry picking. In winter hunters also traveled about 30 miles up the El Dorado River to look for caribou in the Salmon Lake area. They would send smoke signals into the air to herald a successful hunt.

Today the Cape continues to serve as an excellent vantage point for Native seal hunters primarily in the fall as the ice approaches and early spring as leads open up in the ice.

Berry picking is still an important family activity in the Nome area.

▶ Mile 13: Quarry and pier

Habitat: Rocky outcrop, coastal waters

Cape Nome is a massive granitic outcrop that is much more resistant to weathering than surrounding lands. Local Alaska Native corporations quarry the rock, which is trucked or barged to large-scale construction projects up and down the coast. Nome's seawall is built from this granite. Amidst considerable construction or quarry activity, birds continue to nest or roost on the rock faces. The thickly-vegetated slopes attract dense numbers of warbler and sparrow species during the spring nesting season.

Despite the industrial landscape, the rock quarry yields many birding delights.

Peregrine falcon and common raven regularly nest on the quarry ledges. Murres, Kittlitz's murrelet, pigeon guillemot, loons, and pelagic cormorant feed by diving in this deep water area, though ocean swells may make them tricky to see. Brant, eiders, scoters, puffins, gulls, and kittiwakes fly past the Cape at close and offshore distances.

▶ Mile 14: Cape Nome Roadhouse

As you round Cape Nome, the Cape Nome Roadhouse is on the shore-side of the road. Roadhouses once flourished along trails around the state, providing food and shelter for winter travelers who often arrived by dog team or horse-drawn sleigh. The Cape Nome Roadhouse also served as an orphanage after the devastating epidemics of the early 1900s and as a World War II communications base. It is now a privately-owned camp.

Cape Nome Roadhouse

Mile 14 to 34 | Cape Nome to Solomon

Habitat: Ponds, coastal waters, beaches, lagoons

Coastal grasslands & Safety Sound

Leaving Cape Nome, the road passes through the coastal grasslands, dunes, and meadows of a long and narrow barrier island environment. This sandy strip of land divides the protected wetlands and lagoon of Safety Sound from the unprotected marine waters of Norton Sound and the Bering Sea. The close proximity of these waters makes this one of the most dynamic and interesting places for birdlife on the road system. Huge numbers of diverse species arrive at different times to breed and nest, feed throughout the summer, and regroup before migrating south in the fall. The area is named an "Important Bird Area" of North America in recognition of its unique importance for birds.

Meadows and ponds border Safety Sound Lagoon.

Spring and summer at Safety Sound

In May and early June, melt water appears at the mouths of rivers entering the lagoons and shore zones. The early open water and mudflats are critical arrival and feeding sites for large numbers of spring migrant loons, waterfowl, shorebirds, and gulls returning to the area to breed. The shallow waters of Safety Sound warm up to 65 °F in summer, which encourages the growth of abundant eel grass beds and clouds of Chronomid midge flies for many birds and fish to feast on. Most nesting is underway by mid-June and the season quickly gives way to a brief but near continuous summer feast. Birds capitalize on an explosion of insects, plants, and schools of migrating capelin, smelt, herring, and salmon.

Brant and common eiders in large numbers build their down-lined nests on salt grass meadows and islands within protected lagoon waters. Later, the females may be seen with their young. King, spectacled, and Steller's eiders are often associated with large rafts of birds using marine waters in early spring. Tundra swan, Canada goose, snow goose, and sandhill crane arrive in large numbers, with some remaining near the road for the entire summer. Northern pintail, northern shoveler, American wigeon, green-winged teal, greater scaup, long-tailed duck, red-breasted merganser, and other duck species use lagoon waters and often cluster at locations adjacent to the road. Specialty species like gadwall, Eurasian wigeon, and ring-necked and tufted duck are sometimes found by experienced eyes. Loons are particularly prevalent and this the best place to find all five North American species: red-throated, Arctic, Pacific, common, and yellow-billed loons. Shorebirds are represented by vast numbers of western sandpiper nesting in meadow habitat and along the lagoon beaches you can find semiplamated sandpiper, red-necked

Northern shoveler (female)

Pacific loon nest

stint, dunlin, and long-billed dowitcher. Nearby you'll find black turnstone associated with areas at the west end of Safety Sound. In some years Eurasian species like lesser sand-plover and ruff make appearances in this area.

Arctic tern are widely abundant, while Aleutian tern may be found in small colonies at variable locations. Large numbers of glaucous gull and mew gull are interspersed with smaller numbers of Sabine's, glaucous-winged, herring or vega, and slaty-backed gulls. Lapland longspur and savannah sparrow are abundant nesting species among the taller grasses. Peregrine falcon, long-tail jaeger,

Lapland longspur (male)

and parasitic jaeger feed on songbirds and shorebirds. Snowy owl may be nesting around the east end of Safety Sound in areas where patterned ground provides a bit of elevation for dry nesting.

Broad vistas make it possible to spot moose or groups of muskox at great distances as they forage or traverse the flat meadows. Arctic fox venture into this area to feed on birds, eggs, and voles and to scavenge on dead marine mammals that wash ashore. Arctic ground squirrel dig burrows easily in the sandy soils, often choosing a spot by a large piece of driftwood.

Muskox are easy to spot in open meadows.

Early fall at Safety Sound

In August and September, huge flocks of migrating waterfowl and shorebirds gather at Safety Sound prior to departing south. Gyrfalcon come to hunt small and medium-size birds. The coastal forelands serve as a flyway for migrant sandhill crane, and groups that number in the thousands are seen and heard overhead in loud, loose V-formations.

A northern hawk owl perches on an Iditarod trail marker.

Freeze-up at Safety Sound

The lagoon waters become increasingly salty as the fresh water begins to freeze, creating new feeding areas for some marine fish. Saffron cod (locally called tomcod) escape predatory seals by entering the lagoon and seeking shelter under the ice. Seals can't follow because the ice is too thick for them to break open a breathing hole. Residents chip holes in the ice, however, and jig with colorfully-decorated hooks to catch tomcod for freezing, drying, or baking.

Winter tom codding on ice.

Ancient house pits & historical subsistence

The Inupiat have long occupied sites along the barrier beach to fish for salmon and tomcod, hunt seal and waterfowl, and gather greens and berries. On the inland side of the road, the long barrier beach is marked by many shallow, vegetated depressions in the soil: ancient house pit sites approximately 8-to-10-feet across. At one time, these now weatherworn remains of Inupiat summer camps were framed over with driftwood and covered with walrus skins. Residents of the village of Ayasayuk on Cape Nome used them and so did travelers from other winter villages, seeking summer's abundance of waterfowl, eggs, fish, greens, and berries.

These small mounds are the remains of ancient house pits.

Nuuk and contemporary subsistence

The numerous contemporary camps in this area, called Nuuk, are testimony to the unbroken tradition of subsistence hunting, fishing, and gathering. Seals may be seen in spring, basking on the shore-fast ice or popping their heads out of the water in summer. The camps and associated structures provide nesting sites for tree swallow, American robin, and common raven. Sand dunes in the area offer denning sites for Arctic ground squirrel and red fox. The cabins are privately owned, so please don't trespass.

A fish camp on the barrier islands.

Sandhill cranes fly over subsistence camps near Nome.

▶ Mile 22: Safety Sound Roadhouse and Safety Bridge

Habitat: Lagoon, coastal waters, meadow, beaches

The Safety Sound roadhouse still opens in summer to offer travelers shelter from the rain or a cool beverage to wash down the dust. It's closed the rest of the year except for several weeks in March, when it serves as the final checkpoint for the Iditarod Trail Sled Dog Race.

Safety Bridge

The Safety Bridge is a good vantage point to watch changing tides and the movement of large and small fish and their predators. Scan for the bobbing heads of seals attracted by the summer fish runs. They are most likely young spotted seals, which remain in coastal waters for the summer rather than follow the ice edge north. Salmon enter through the channel during certain light, tide, and wind conditions. Birds feed on escaping salmon smolt or arriving capelin and herring. They include large numbers of eiders, scoters, gulls, kittiwakes, and terns. Look for herring eggs near the lagoon entrance among the mounds of eel grass that wash up along the beach in spring. On the lagoon side, shorebirds and gulls collect on the extensive mud flats at low tide. Take time to search for rare species that mix with the large numbers of common species.

▶ Mile 22: Alaska Maritime National Wildlife Refuge pullout

Immediately after the bridge, a turn-off on the inland side of the road leads to several interpretive signs and a boardwalk for wildlife viewing.

▶ Mile 28–32: Bonanza Channel

Habitat: Estuary

Safety Lagoon slowly narrows and mixes with wetlands, ponds, and the Bonanza River estuary. Thousands of tundra swan move through this area on their spring migration. Breeding swans move on to upland ponds to nest and raise their young, while non-breeding birds may remain all summer. In the fall, parts of the lagoon and Solomon River wetlands turn white with huge groups of swans preparing for fall migration.

Tundra swans gathering on lagoon waters.

▶ Mile 32-34: Bonanza Bridge to Solomon

Habitat: Wetlands, coastal waters

Western sandpipers

In the fall, people fish for tomcod from the bridge. Deep diving ducks feed in the channel depths of the Bonanza River. Sandhill crane feed on berries, plant shoots, roots, insects, and even small rodents. Red-throated loon and, less commonly, Pacific loon float the waters. Northern pintail, the most abundant waterfowl on the Seward Peninsula, and second-ranked long-tailed duck are primary species in the area near the bridge. Also, look for good numbers of shorebirds (red-necked phalarope, red phalarope, western sandpiper, least sandpiper, rock sandpiper, dunlin, and long-bill dowitcher) among the small ponds just north of the bridge.

▶ Mile 33: The Last Train to Nowhere

Just across Bonanza Bridge, three rusty steam locomotives and some rolling stock lie sinking into the water-logged tundra. Dubbed "The Last Train to Nowhere," they are all that remain of a dream to build the most extensive and prosperous rail system on the Seward Peninsula. In the early 1900s, Chicago investors backed construction of the Council City & Solomon River Railroad in an effort to link the region's major mining centers by rail. But as the gold rush faded, the project became mired in debt and after five years of construction, the line extended only 35 miles. The project was abandoned in 1907 and the locomotives left to deteriorate. Today the popular attraction is equipped with viewing platforms and interpretive signs.

The Last Train to Nowhere

Habitat: Tundra meadow, river valley, human-modified, side slopes, inland cliffs, dwarf tundra

The road travels through several different habitats as it climbs toward the summit at Skookum Pass. Scan the slopes and willow bottoms for possible sightings of grizzly, moose, reindeer, and muskox and check rock outcrops and cliff faces for raptor nests, using the splashes of orange lichen or whitewash as a guide.

▶ Mile 34: Solomon

The town of Solomon has had several names and locations since the Fish River tribe established a fishing and hunting camp called Amutach on a sandbar between the Bonanza and Solomon Rivers. In 1899, when gold was discovered in the gravels of the Solomon River, a mining boomtown sprang up on the site with a post office, several saloons, a railroad terminal, a ferry dock, and over 2,000 residents. Thirteen large dredges worked the Solomon River.

An old mining dredge provides a platform for a stick nest.

In 1913 a ferocious storm destroyed the town and residents relocated upstream to the recently abandoned town of Dickson, which has since been washed away. As mining waned, Solomon became a predominately Native village and residents relied on reindeer herding and subsistence. The 1918 flu epidemic took a tremendous toll. In 1939 the village was moved to its current location on Jerusalem Hill to avoid the river's annual flooding.

Solomon Roadhouse

Heading north, the Solomon Roadhouse, which housed the store and post office, is on your right while the recently restored school house is on your left. Other buildings in the area are private cabins.

Dredges on the Solomon River

The 13 dredges that operated on the Solomon River and its tributaries at one time or another altered the condition of the riverbed, sometimes eliminating the pools and riffles necessary for salmon spawning. The undredged section of river along the first four miles of road offers a comparison to the dredged portions upriver.

Wandering tattler

Areas where tall felt-leaf willows grow closest to the main branch of the river are free of permafrost and the lush vegetation attracts many species of songbirds. Red-breasted merganser and harlequin duck float the river. Glaucous gull often rest on gravel bars and American dipper, wandering tattler, and spotted sandpiper frequent river banks and islands.

Mining and fish

Driving northward, piles of gravel tailings start to appear along the river—the remains of earlier mining activity on the Solomon River. Typically, salmon are most affected by mining because the disturbance stirs up fine sediments, which are carried downstream. Settling on the river bed in a process called "concretion," they coat the fish eggs that were laid in the silt and choke off their supply of oxygen and nutrients. Placer mining techniques now call for settling ponds, where the water is held until the sediments drop out and only then returned to the river. Natural systems heal somewhat over time and salmon still return to spawn in the Solomon River, although not in the same numbers they once did.

The gravel tailings on the riverbank to the right show the arcing sweep of a dredge's boom.

Mining activity also thawed some of the ground in the river valley, encouraging a more recent growth of cottonwoods.

▶ Mile 39: Shovel Creek

Beaver diving.

Shovel Creek passes under the road through a double culvert before it enters the Solomon River. A year-round spring that feeds the creek near the road keeps the water from freezing in winter. This attracts dippers, beaver, mink, and otter and encourages the growth of cottonwoods. The spring-fed creek also offers a moderate amount of spawning habitat for pink, chum, and coho salmon in late July and August. Dolly Varden are present but few Arctic grayling.

▶ Mile 39.5: Lee's Dredge

Habitat: Human-modified, ponds

Lee's Dredge, the last dredge to work the Solomon River, was operated by the Lee family until the 1960s. It now provides nesting platforms for raptors and ravens. You may see green-winged teal and phalaropes feeding in the dredge pond and songbirds in the surrounding willows.

▶ Mile 40.4: Old side road to Solomon River overlook

Habitat: Cliff face, river valley

The overlook is a good vantage point from which to look for wildlife.

An old road bed leading to a Solomon River overlook is a good spot to look for salmon, Dolly Varden, and Arctic grayling in late July and August. Chum salmon rarely spawn beyond here as dredging took out the pools and riffles they seek. Coho salmon spawn a little farther upriver. Say's phoebe will launch from its nest on a secluded ledge or crevice on the cliff face to catch insects flying above the river. Northern shrike, harlequin duck, spotted sandpiper, and wandering tattler are seen from this vantage point. In some years, the cliff is occupied by common raven, rough-legged hawk, or other raptors so be careful your presence does not disturb nesting birds. The side road reconnects with Council Road at Mile 41.

▶ Mile 42: Solomon Bridge/Big Hurrah Creek

In 1904 a telephone line ran from Nome to the railroad terminus at Dickson, to the mining camps up Big Hurrah Creek, and on to Council. For one brief summer, parcels could be mailed to any point in the U.S. and money orders sent worldwide. The Council City & Solomon River Railroad also ran past, offering miners a one-hour trip to the coast. Grizzlies, moose, muskox, and reindeer are frequently sighted between the creek and East Fork Bridge.

A northern shrike dives for a moth. This predatory songbird also feeds on small birds and mammals.

▶ Mile 45: **East Fork Bridge**

Habitat: River valley, side slopes, human-modified

Approaching the East Fork of Solomon River, a wide pull-off on the left is an excellent place to park and scan the slopes and river valley for wildlife. Northern wheatear and American pipit frequent the rocky slopes nearby. Cliff swallow often build nests on the bridge supports, and ravens and raptors occasionally nest in the area. This elevated view of the river makes it easy to find red-breasted merganser, harlequin duck, tattlers, and gulls.

A cow moose and her calf keeping close to the willowed streambeds in spring.

Council City and Solomon River Railroad

Area railroads also included the Nome Arctic Railway: a narrow gauge rail accessing mines north of Council.

Look for a straight line of vegetation cutting across the side slope on the opposite side of the river. This is the old railroad grade that was part of the Council City & Solomon River Railroad . The plan was to build the track up the East Fork of the Solomon River to mining centers at Ruby and the Casadepaga River, then down to the Niukluk River and Council City. Before the project was abandoned in 1907, a train ran past twice a week on its way to Penelope Creek and the Casadepaga River. The old grade catches and holds rain and snow, and the added moisture has allowed willow and other plants to grow tall, attracting songbirds, small rodents, and furbearers.

A weasel in its winter white pellage.

A braided riverbed – more moose, fewer fish

Reindeer cross the tundra above a braided riverbed.

Below its confluence with the East Fork, the riverbed of the Solomon River is braided and constantly changing. This seasonal scouring reduces vegetation and prevents establishment of deep pools where aquatic insects can over-winter, thus reducing the number of fish. It also prevents the establishment of pools and riffles needed by spawning salmon. The frequent washouts create a constant growth of new willows, however, providing a renewable food source for moose.

▶ Mile 48: Raptor nest

Habitat: Rocky outcrop

The rocky outcrop across the Solomon River usually hosts an active golden eagle nest. Look for a huge tower of sticks and splashes of whitewash and orange lichen in the vicinity of the nest and surrounding perching sites. Built by eagles and added onto in successive years, the nest is distinctive for its large size, construction, and shape. When not occupied

Gyrfalcon chicks

Rough-legged hawk chick

by eagles, the large nest may be used by gyrfalcons. Smaller nests of rough-legged hawks or common ravens may be elsewhere on the cliff. If you don't see a nest, check for a pile of sticks on the ground below. The winds or snow loads sometimes cause nests to collapse. When this happens, the eagles often rebuild.

▶ Mile 53: Skookum Pass pull-out

Habitat: Side slopes, dwarf tundra

A small parking area at the highest point is an excellent place to pull off the road safely and explore the alpine tundra. On a clear day this high point offers sweeping views of Norton Sound to the southeast and the westernmost boreal forest to the north. The open country can be a good place to spot moose, muskox, or grizzlies. Caribou, normally present in winter, are sometimes seen in summer too. You are more likely to see reindeer, however, which are distinguished by their pinto coloration, short legs, and the occasional ear tag. Wolf and wolverine use this alpine habitat too, but sightings are rare as both species have low population densities and huge home ranges.

The road descends from Skookum Pass headed for Council.

The parking area offers a particularly good view of solifluction lobes on side slopes caused when moisture-laden topsoil overlying permafrost slides extremely slowly downhill in waves.

Wolverines may be present in the area, but they are elusive and rarely spotted.

Mile 53 to 72 — Skookum Pass to Council

Habitat: Dwarf tundra, side slopes, boreal forest, tundra meadow, river valley

It's not long before the first spruce trees begin to appear on the landscape. The mountains you have just crossed tend to separate the moderating effects of the coastal Bering Sea climate—cool summers and windy but moderate winters—from the extremes of an interior climate—hot summers and deeply cold, calm winters. The different climate regime

Soon after Skookum Pass, the first spruce trees appear.

and the presence of spruce forest, deciduous trees like birch and aspen, very tall willow, and alder shrubs mean you are likely to encounter many new bird species

Three-toed woodpecker

along this section of the road. While some species like golden eagle, glaucous gull, northern shrike, swallows, raven, sparrows, and warblers straddle boreal and tundra habitats, don't be surprised to find any of the following birds along the last 20 miles of the road to Council: spruce grouse, bald eagle, osprey, northern goshawk, great horned owl, northern hawk owl, boreal owl, belted kingfisher, downy woodpecker, three-toed woodpecker, gray jay, black-capped chickadee, boreal chickadee, ruby-crowned kinglet, varied thrush, Bohemian waxwing, yellow-rumped warbler, dark-eyed junco, rusty blackbird, pine grosbeak, and white-winged crossbill.

Boreal owl

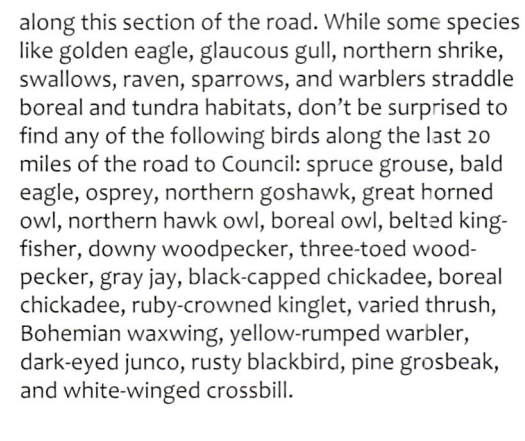

Black-capped chickadee

Belted kingfisher (female)

Varied thrush (fledgling)

The balancing act between moose and bears

Moose numbers along the Fox River and Niukluk River drainages were robust during the 1980s, but a series of deep snow winters and too few willows to sustain the population led to a population crash in the early 1990s. Since then the willows have recovered but not the moose, whose numbers continued to be depressed as recently as 2010—likely the result of a healthy grizzly population regularly preying on moose calves.

▶ Mile 68: Fox River Bridge

Habitat: River valley, boreal forest

Cow moose and calf crossing the river.

Descending into terrain increasingly dominated by trees and willows, you are more likely to see a moose than a muskox. In late summer grizzlies feed on spawning chum salmon below the Fox River bridge. Salmon carcasses also attract red fox, gulls, and common ravens. Both abandoned and active beaver lodges and dams are found along the Fox River drainage. Dolly Varden, Arctic grayling, and chum and pink salmon can be seen from the bridge.

Downstream, the narrow, swift-flowing river is hemmed in by dense vegetation. Spotted sandpiper may be seen on a sand bar on the east side of the road and belted kingfisher burrow into the riverbanks to nest.

▶ Mile 68 – 72: To the end of Council Road

Habitat: Tundra meadow, wet tundra

Hares are thought to derive nutritional benefits from the minerals in roadbeds.

The final section of the Council Road traverses habitat that is unlike any other along the road system—open parklands dotted with clusters of tall spruce trees. Northern harrier hunt voles, shrews, and lemmings in the meadows. In years of abundance, you may see snowshoe hares licking minerals from the roadbed. Lynx also frequent the area when hares are abundant. Moose feed on aquatic plants in lowland ponds.

▶ Mile 72: Council area

Habitat: River valley, boreal forest, human-modified

Unlike other braided rivers along the road system, the Niukluk River flows along a single broad channel. A large colony of cliff swallow inhabits the cliff banks downstream while tree swallow nest in aspen cavities and nest boxes put up by Council residents.

Niukluk River

Osprey, which nest downstream, may be spotted flying over the river. Bald eagle are also associated with the river and nest at the Fish River confluence. In the sparse forest around Council, red squirrels gather and cache green spruce cones for winter, marten are elusive spruce tree dwellers, porcupines feed on the inner bark of spruce, and least and short-tailed weasels use old buildings for nesting and denning. On rare occasions, grizzlies, moose, and wolves wander through town.

River plants find a toehold among the boulders.

A number of summer camps are located downstream on the Niukluk and Fish Rivers where people fish for chum and coho salmon. Farther down the Fish River, Chinook and pink salmon may be found and occasionally, sockeye salmon. Dolly Varden, Arctic grayling, and whitefish are also present in the Niukluk, as are burbot when they prepare to spawn in fall time. Northern pike are available farther downstream in the Fish River.

River crossing warning! The road ends at the Niukluk River but most of the community of Council lies on the other side. River crossings should be made only in a high-clearance 4WD vehicle under the direction of a local person who knows the route. The expense and embarrassment of getting stuck are not pleasant. Wading across the hip-deep waters is generally not possible.

All buildings, boats, and property on both sides of the river are privately-owned. Please do not disturb or trespass.

A brief history of Council

In September 1897 Daniel B. Libby—having observed some good gold prospects on the Niukluk River some 30 years earlier when he worked for the Western Union Telegraph Expedition—returned to try his luck in the Fish River area. Libby and his group found promising amounts of gold and, in the spring of 1898, began construction of a mining camp they called Council City.

The road ends at the Niukluk River across from Council. Do not try to ford the river without assistance.

Word spread and hundreds of stampeders in Southeast Alaska, disappointed to find the Klondike riches were already staked and claimed, headed north. A trading post, saloons, and boarding houses sprang up in Council City, but many prospectors moved on to Anvil City (later re-named Nome) that winter when news broke of the big strike by the "Three Lucky Swedes."

Chum and pink salmon drying at a fish camp along the river.

Nevertheless, mining paid off for those who had established the best claims in Council and the town persisted. Today, it remains a popular summer retreat for residents of Nome and others with fish camps on the Niukluk and Fish Rivers. About 20 of the old buildings remain and remnants of mining equipment are scattered about.

Locals who enjoy the warm summers have built summer homes and planted gardens. A few hardy souls occasionally winter in Council. Others make extended trips out by snowmachine and run active trap lines.

Many Council residents put up nest boxes for tree swallows.

City of Nome Walking Tour

Norton Sound

N

| 0 | 0.25 | 0.5 |

Miles

1 East End Park

2 Front Street Satellite Dish

3 Second Avenue

4 Nome Harbor

5 Dry Creek Estuary

6 Cemetery Hill

7 Cemetery Ponds

8 Monofil Ponds

9 West Beach

Nome Walking Tour

Birding is a rewarding experience in Nome, even in and around town.

Nome offers several bird watching opportunities in the heart of town or at nearby peripheral areas, which are all accessible within walking distances of no more than two miles.

East End Park/Swanberg Dredge

These stops on the east edge of Nome (described in more detail in the Council Road section) offer freshwater ponds adjacent to the marine water coastline that attract a wide variety of spring migrant waterbirds and shorebirds as the ice is melting in late May and early June. The area is worth checking regularly because arriving species often make a short stop before moving inland. By mid-summer, early departing shorebirds gather to feed and fatten before migration.

A good field guide to birds is a valuable resource.

Front Street satellite dish

Near the center of town along the beachline, a large satellite communication dish regularly attracts nesting common raven. In early March they start building and refurbishing their nest on the supporting cross-arms. By May the parent birds are standing guard or delivering food to ever-hungry nestlings. The young usually leave the nest in late June or July and become a raucous traveling family with an

Front Street is a busy place to raise a family.

ever-expanding range. The adults may accompany them and be protective, especially against gulls or other avian predators. You can tell which are the young because their flight and tail feathers are of a uniform length. Adult ravens have missing and uneven feathers due to variable growth after feathers are lost during the molt.

Second Avenue

In winter between October and mid-April, buntings cluster close to bird feeders in the center of town along Second Ave. A mix of McKay's and snow buntings will perch on utility wires in congregations of up to 100 birds, close enough for viewers to see the subtle differences in these small snowbirds. Chickadees, redpolls, and sometimes a dark-eyed junco also come to the center of town, most often when fall is eclipsing into winter and again in late winter when days are growing longer and spring is in the air.

Birdseed draws in snow (l) and McKay's (r) buntings. Come spring, the McKay's bunting moves on to Bering Sea islands to breed.

Nome harbor

The Nome harbor (viewed in the distance from Anvil Mountain) is rich with birdlife.

Look for loons, mergansers, gulls, terns, and kittiwakes where the Snake River flows into the Nome harbor area, either close to the beach or in the salt and fresh water mixing zone. When ice covers the harbor during the spring thaw, the plume of river melt attracts a mixture of arriving species seeking open water near the coast. Many birds stay in the area throughout the summer, making this an important local hot spot for birdlife.

Dry Creek estuary

Pectoral sandpiper

Skirt the harbor and walk toward the west side of the port area along Seppala Avenue, and you'll cross the culvert where Dry Creek flows into the harbor. Upstream is a wide area of lowland vegetation. This area is subject to salt water intrusion during wind driven high tides, affecting the wetland habitat as it reaches the side slopes of tundra and willow shrubs. Puddle ducks forage and nest here. Look for shorebirds and other species as well.

Cemetery hill

The west flank of Dry Creek leads to the Nome Cemetery on a small rounded hill. The narrow cemetery roads cross tundra and willow shrub habitats that dominate the area due to the slight rise in elevation. While being respectful of the grave markers, search for northern shrike, bohemian waxwing, or black-capped chickadee and enjoy the common tundra bird species as well. Don't be surprised if an eastern yellow wagtail flying overhead escorts you through the area.

Northern shrike

Dredge pond

Bordering the cemetery hill to the north, at the intersection of Center Creek Road and the west extension of the Nome ByPass Road, a large man-made pond from placer mining operations that is slowly becoming vegetated is a good place to find a few species of nesting waterbirds. Red-necked grebe, glaucous gull, greater scaup, northern shoveler, and green-winged teal may be found near the center and edges of the pond. Over the years some unusual species, such as spectacled eider, long-toed stint, and other shorebird specialties, have been observed at this location as well.

Northern shoveler (male)

Monofil ponds

Monofil ponds viewed from Anvil Mountain.

About a mile further north on Center Creek Road, a wetland meadow lies west of the old Nome dump, which is now used as a monofil area for large bulky refuse that does not belong in the sanitary landfill. The monofil area might attract ravens or gulls, but the real gem is the wetland meadow interspersed with remnant structures from earlier mining activity. Red-necked phalarope, pintail,

teal, and scaup are often floating on the pond near the road, and geese, gulls, and terns are common in more distant locations. When it's warm out and insects are flying, an abundance of swallows forage just above the water and meadow. Rusty blackbird feeds and nests in the area, so be on the lookout for a dark-bodied, long-tailed bird walking the perimeter of the ponds.

Rusty blackbird (female)

West beach

Returning south of the road to the airport (Seppala Avenue) and west of the Nome port, the beach front area offers a good view of the marine waters of Norton Sound and the barge docking area built of quarried rock from Cape Nome. Depending on the season, the open ocean view will be punctuated with passing flocks of eiders, brant, scoters, murres, auklets, cormorants, and other seabirds.

Surf scoters (males)

Hugging the breakwater rocks or near the beach, look for several species of loons, harlequin duck, and red-breasted merganser. Terns may pester you as you walk the beach and gulls of varied species will launch into flight. Be watchful for Aleutian tern sometimes mixed with Arctic tern in this area.

Nome Area Roadways
Bird List

A - Abundant: numerous in all proper habitats
C - Common: regular in most proper habitats
U - Uncommon: usually present in small numbers
R - Rare: regular in small numbers
- Casual or accidental: recorded no more than a few times

- Spring (Mar-May)
- Summer (June- Aug)
- Fall (Sept-Nov)
- Winter (Dec-Feb)

✔ Bird Species	Spring	Summer	Fall	Winter
Gr White-fronted Goose	C	C	C	
Emperor Goose	U	U	U	
Snow Goose	C	C	C	
Brant	C	A	C	
Cackling Goose	U	C	U	
Canada Goose	C	A	C	
Tundra Swan	C	A	A	
Gadwall	R	R	R	
Eurasian Wigeon	R	R	R	
American Wigeon	C	A	A	
Mallard	R	R	R	
Blue-winged Teal		#		
Northern Shoveler	C	A	C	
Northern Pintail	A	A	A	
Green-winged Teal	C	A	C	
Canvasback	R	R	R	
Redhead		#		
Ring-necked Duck		#		
Tufted Duck		#		
Greater Scaup	C	A	A	
Lesser Scaup	R	R	R	
Steller's Eider	R	R	R	
Spectacled Eider	R	R	R	
King Eider	R	R	R	R

✔ Bird Species	Spring	Summer	Fall	Winter
Common Eider	A	A	A	R
Harlequin Duck	C	A	C	
Surf Scoter	C	C	C	
White-winged Scoter	C	C	C	
Black Scoter	C	C	C	
Long-tailed Duck	A	A	C	R
Bufflehead		#		
Common Goldeneye	R	R		
Smew		#		
Common Merganser	R	R	R	
Red-breasted Merganser	C	A	C	
Spruce Grouse	R	R	R	R
Willow Ptarmigan	A	A	A	A
Rock Ptarmigan	C	C	C	C
Red-throated Loon	C	A	C	
Arctic Loon	R	R	R	
Pacific Loon	C	C	C	
Common Loon	R	R	R	
Yellow-billed Loon	R	R	R	
Horned Grebe	R	R	R	
Red-necked Grebe	R	C	R	
Northern Fulmar	R	R	R	
Fork-tailed Storm-Petrel		#		
Pelagic Cormorant	C	C	C	

✔	Bird Species				
	Turkey Vulture		#		
	Osprey	R	R	R	
	Bald Eagle	R	R	R	
	Northern Harrier	C	C	R	
	Northern Goshawk	R	R	R	R
	Rough-legged Hawk	C	A	C	
	Golden Eagle	C	C	C	R
	American Kestrel		#		
	Merlin	R	R	R	
	Gyrfalcon	C	C	C	C
	Peregrine Falcon	R	R	R	
	Sandhill Crane	C	A	A	
	Black-bellied Plover	R	R	R	
	American Golden-Plover	C	A	C	
	Pacific Golden-Plover	C	A	C	
	Lesser Sand-Plover	R	R		
	Common Ringed Plover		#		
	Semipalmated Plover	C	A	C	
	Eurasian Dotterel		#		
	Terek Sandpiper		#		
	Spotted Sandpiper	C	C	C	
	Solitary Sandpiper	R	R	R	
	Gray-tailed Tattler		#		
	Wandering Tattler	C	C	R	
	Lesser Yellowlegs	R	R	R	
	Wood Sandpiper		#		
	Whimbrel	C	A	A	
	Bristle-thighed Curlew	R	R	R	
	Black-tailed Godwit		#		
	Hudsonian Godwit		#		
	Bar-tailed Godwit	C	A	C	
	Marbled Godwit		#		
	Ruddy Turnstone	C	C	C	
	Black Turnstone	C	A	C	
	Surfbird	R	R	R	
	Red Knot	R	R	R	

✔	Bird Species				
	Sanderling	R	R	R	
	Semipalmated Sandpiper	C	A	C	
	Western Sandpiper	A	A	A	
	Red-necked Stint	R	R	R	
	Long-toed Stint		#		
	Least Sandpiper	R	R	R	
	Baird's Sandpiper	R	R	R	
	Pectoral Sandpiper	R	R	R	
	Rock Sandpiper	R	R	R	
	Dunlin	C	A	A	
	Stilt Sandpiper	R	R	R	
	Ruff		#		
	Long-bill Dowitcher	C	A	A	
	Wilson's Snipe	A	A	C	
	Red-necked Phalarope	C	A	A	
	Red Phalarope	R	R	R	
	Black-legged Kittiwake	A	A	A	
	Ivory Gull	#	#	#	#
	Sabine's Gull	R	C	R	
	Bonaparte's Gull	R	R	R	
	Ross's Gull	#	#		
	Mew Gull	A	A	A	
	Ring-billed Gull		#		
	Herring Gull	R	R	R	
	Slaty-backed Gull	R	R	R	
	Glaucous-winged Gull	C	C	C	
	Glaucous Gull	A	A	C	R
	Aleutian Tern	R	C	R	
	Common Tern		#		
	Arctic Tern	C	A	A	
	Pomarine Jaeger	R	R	R	
	Parasitic Jaeger	C	C	C	
	Long-tailed Jaeger	A	A	A	
	Dovekie	#	#		
	Common Murre	R	R	R	
	Thick-billed Murre	C	C	C	R

✔	Bird Species	🟩 🟧 🟪 🟦
	Black Guillemot	R R R
	Pigeon Guillemot	R R R
	Kittlitz's Murrelet	R R R R
	Parakeet Auklet	# #
	Least Auklet	# #
	Crested Auklet	# #
	Horned Puffin	R C C
	Tufted Puffin	R R R
	Great Horned Owl	R R R R
	Snowy Owl	R R R R
	Northern Hawk Owl	R R R R
	Short-eared Owl	R C C
	Boreal Owl	R R R R
	Rufous Hummingbird	#
	Belted Kingfisher	R R R
	Downy Woodpecker	R R R R
	Western Wood-Pewee	R R
	Alder Flycatcher	R R
	Say's Phoebe	R C C
	Northern Shrike	C C C C
	Gray Jay	C C C C
	Common Raven	A A A A
	Horned Lark	R R R
	Tree Swallow	C A C
	Northern Rough-winged Swallow	#
	Bank Swallow	C A C
	Cliff Swallow	C A C
	Black-capped Chickadee	C C C C
	Boreal Chickadee	R R R R
	American Dipper	R R R R
	Ruby-crowned Kinglet	R R
	Arctic Warbler	R C C
	Siberian Rubythroat	#
	Bluethroat	R R R
	Northern Wheatear	R C C
	Gray-cheeked Thrush	C A A

✔	Bird Species	🟩 🟧 🟪 🟦
	Hermit Thrush	R R R
	American Robin	C A A
	Varied Thrush	R R R
	Eastern Yellow Wagtail	R A C
	White Wagtail	R R R
	Red-throated Pipit	R R R
	American Pipit	C C C
	Bohemian Waxwing	R R R R
	Lapland Longspur	C A A
	Snow Bunting	C A C A
	McKay's Bunting	C C A
	Orange-crowned Warbler	R A C
	Yellow Warbler	R A C
	Yellow-rumped Warbler	R C C
	Blackpoll Warbler	R A A
	Northern Waterthrush	R A A
	Wilson's Warbler	R A A
	American Tree Sparrow	R A A
	Savannah Sparrow	R A A
	Fox Sparrow	R A A
	Lincoln's Sparrow	R R R
	White-crowned Sparrow	R A A
	Golden-crowned Sparrow	R A A
	Dark-eyed Junco	R R R R
	Rusty Blackbird	R R R
	Brambling	#
	Gray-crowned Rosy-Finch	R R R R
	Pine Grosbeak	R R R R
	White-winged Crossbill	R R R R
	Common Redpoll	A A C
	Hoary Redpoll	C C R
	Eurasian Bullfinch	# #
	Hawfinch	#
	House Sparrow	#

Planning your visit and other resources

Information on car rentals, accomodations, and other local services

Nome Convention and Visitors Bureau
Mailing address: P.O. Box 240, Nome, AK 99762
Physical address: 301 Front Street
Phone: (907) 443-6555; Fax: (907) 443-5832
E-mail: visit@mynomealaska.com
Website: www.visitnomealaska.com

Wildlife information

Learn more about wildlife and staying safe in bear country at the Alaska Department of Fish and Game (ADF&G) website at www.wildlifeviewing.alaska.gov.

Road conditions

For information about road conditions, including closures, contact the Alaska State Troopers at (800) 443-2835 or the Alaska Department of Transportation at (907) 443-3444.

Land status and private property

The road system crosses lands owned and managed by the State of Alaska, the Bureau of Land Management (BLM), U.S. Fish and Wildlife Service (USFWS), and private landholders, including local and regional Native corporations. State and BLM-managed lands are available for public use but there may be some restrictions or need for a permit or authorization for your planned activity. Privately-owned lands, including Native corporation lands, are typically not posted. If you are planning activities on privately-owned lands, other than viewing from the road, you need permission from the owner. The BLM staff at the Federal Building in Nome, (907) 443-2177, can help you identify land ownership and provide you with contact information for private landholders. Interactive maps are available online at the Alaska Mapper website at http://mapper.landrecords.info/.

A permit is required to access the Pilgrim Hot Springs property off Kougarok Road. Contact the Bering Straits Native Corporation at 110 Front Street in Nome at (907) 443-5252, the Nome Visitor's Center, or the Aurora Inn.

Sick or injured animals

If you find a sick, injured, or seemingly orphaned animal, leave the animal alone and report your concerns to the ADF&G office in Nome at (907) 443-2271 or the Alaska Wildlife Trooper at (907) 443-2429. The ADF&G and the Marine Advisory Program at (907) 443-2397 would appreciate reports of all marine mammals whether resting, sick, stranded, or dead.

Vehicles in streams

It is illegal to drive any motorized vehicle (truck, car, ATV, etc) in a salmon spawning stream. This applies to all of the streams on the Nome road system with the exception of several traditional fords where it is permitted to cross such as the

Niukluk River at Council. For a complete list of traditional ford locations, contact the Nome Fish & Game office at 103 E. Front Street. Ford locations are also listed at the ADF&G website: http://www.adfg.alaska.gov/index.cfm?adfg=uselicense.gpcrossing#seward

Fishing

This guidebook does not cover fishing regulations. Please contact the ADF&G Nome office, at 907-443-5167 or check online at: regulations.adfg.alaska.gov.

Acknowledgments

The authors and review team would like to thank John Coady, retired ADF&G Regional Supervisor, for his conceptual vision, impetus, and steadfast support for writing a road-based guide to wildlife for the Nome road system. The Alaska Department of Fish and Game would like to acknowledge the many community members who reviewed this text and provided invaluable suggestions. Their insights and expert knowledge are greatly appreciated. Our thanks are extended to: Austin Ahmasuk, Richard Beneville, Brian Bourdon, Carl and Ginny Emmons, Rose Fosdick, Matt Ganley, Eva Menadelook, Laura Samuelson, Marsha and Mike Sloan, Tom Sparks, Dan Stang, and Alice Sullivan. We are also grateful to the following organizations whose staff and/or members reviewed relevant sections of the guide: Bureau of Land Management, Carrie M. McLain Memorial Museum, Kawerak Eskimo Heritage Program, Reindeer Herders Association, Bering Straits Native Corporation, the Native Village Corporations and Tribes of Nome, Teller, King Island, and Solomon. Our thanks also to ADF&G staff Patti Harper, Riley Woodford, and Meghan Nedwick for their editorial assistance. The National Park Service, Bering Land Bridge Preserve, graciously provided staff and a vehicle to tour the roads.

Photography Credits

©Alaska Department of Fish and Game (ADF&G): pgs. 4 – moose calf, 14 – fingerling, 15 – foxes, 18 – chum salmon, 41 – sow and cubs, 75 – salmon carcass, 77 – char, 91 – boxed muskox. **Peter Bente:** pgs. 5 – watching muskox, 28 – stick nest, 71 – bunting, 87 – cotton grass fields, 93 -Moon Mt., 94 – Tisuk River, 95 – gold dredge, 107 – raptor nest, 132 – swans, 134 – stick nest & roadhouse, 137 – moose, 146 – buntings & harbor. **Travis Booms:** pgs. 61 – gyrfalcon chicks, 62 – gyrfalcon, 138 – gyrfalcon chicks. **Jim Dau:** 17 – bull moose. **Karla Hart:** pgs. 6 – electric fences, 80 – milepost, 115 – sockeye, 118 – Coffee Dome, 127 – rock quarry, 133 – sandpipers, 145 – window sign & birders. **Mark Henspeter:** pg. 68 – raven. **John Hyde:** pg. 35 – bull moose. **Lauri Jemison:** pg. 53 – sea lion. **Mark Keech:** pg. 35 – twin moose. **Lloyd Lowry:** pg. 49 – ribbon seal. **Jody Lozori:** pg. 78 – whitefish. **Ken Marsh:** pgs. 43 – marten, 75 – coho salmon, 77 – pike. **Phil Mooney:** pg. 140 – thrush. **Beth Peluso:** pgs. 26 – forget-me-not & azalea, 31 – squirrel, 32 – Anvil Mt antenna, 84 – Anvil antenna, 142 – Niukluk River, 148 – ponds. **Kate Persons:** pg. 27 – rocky outcrop. **Sue Steinacher:** pgs. 1 – tern, 3 – woman at lake, 4 – bear tracks, 8 – rhododendrons, 9 – mountain valley, 12 – beach, 15 – lagoons, 19 – ponds, 21 – tundra, 23 – side slopes, 25 – dwarf tundra, 26 – harebell & mt. avens & glacier avens, 28 – hawk chicks, 29 – spruce trees, 31 – rock face, 32 – swallow nest, 40 – muskox, 59 – ptarmigan tracks, 66 – jaeger, 74 – salmon drying, 81 – photographer, 84 – rhododendron, 85 – blueberry comb, 86 – canoeing, 87 – cotton grass heads, 88 – Penny River, 89 – House Rock & pink salmon, 90 – Sinuk River, 92 – King Island, 94 – mushroom, 95 – muskox tracks, 96 – fireweed & Teller, 97 – beach greens, 99 – antlers, 103 – fish eggs, 104 – Dexter bypass, 105 – railroad tracks, 106 – beaver dam & aster, 107 – Cape Horn, 109 – Grand Central, 110 – aerial Kigs, 111 – Salmon Lake, 112 – reindeer, 114 – pingo, 116 – sandhill cranes, 122 – slush ice, 125 – Cape Nome, 126 – clouds & alders, 128 – lagoons, 130 – ice fishing, 131 – house pits & fish camp, 133 – Last Train, 135 – river, 136 – overlook, 138 – reindeer, 139 – Skookum Pass & road, 141 – hare, 142 – plants, 143 – Council Rd. end. **Anne Sutton:** pgs. 13 – reindeer, 21 – reindeer, 34 – reindeer, 38 – muskox fur, 45 – squirrel, 71 – sparrow, 73 – bear, 80 – hill, 85 – Dexter bypass, 86 – windmills, 88 – Sledge Island, 90 – milepost marker, 91 – Singatuk, 93 – trail markers, 97 – Teller, 98 – drying rack, 99 – processing plant, 102 – Nome River Valley, 110 – campground & cub track, 111 – Pilgrim River Valley, , 113 – Pilgrim road & Hot Springs, 114 – Pilgrim church, 115 – Pilgrim bridge, 117 – Kuzitrin bridge, 119 – airstrip, 123 – modern dredge & Swanberg Dredge, 127 – berry pickers, 128 – roadhouse, 135 – tattler, 143 – fish camp. **Mike Taras:** pgs. 24 – weasel tracks, 46 – vole tunnel, 47 – shrew, 83 – moose tracks. **Kim Titus:** pgs. 30 – jay, 119 – nest, 139 – wolverine. **Jack Whitman:** pg. 140 – boreal owl.

©Alaska Salmon Marketing Institute: pgs. 73 & 74 – salmon, 75 – 2 coho.

©Cornell Lab of Ornithology: pg. 22 – whimbrel.

National Oceanic & Atmospheric Administration: pgs. 48 – ringed seal, 51 – porpoise.

U.S. Bureau of Ocean Energy Management: pg. 13 – beluga whales.

U.S. Fish and Wildlife Service: pgs. 20 – phalarope, 50 – walrus, 73 – fish eggs, 149 – swan. **Erwin and Peggy Bauer:** pg. 29 – marten. **F. Deines:** pg. 66 – Aleutian terns. **Donna Dewhurst: pg.** 116 – grebe. **Nathan Graff:** pg. 67 – owl. **Liz Labunski:** pg. 48 – bearded seal. **James Leupold: pg.** 94 – fox sparrow. **Suzanne Miller:** pg. 52 – polar bear. **Anne Morkill:** pg. 67 – murres & puffin.

U.S. Geological Survey/Robert Gill: pg. 55 – godwits.

©Bob Armstrong: pgs. 13 – Arctic tern, 20 – otter scat, 22 – vole, 30 – porcupine, 43 – otter, 44 – porcupine, 43 – short-tailed weasel, 45 – beaver, 47 – lemming, 57 – diving duck, 64 – snipe, 66 – Arctic terns, 79 – capelin, 92 – horned lark, 103 – raven, 108 – dipper, 135 – beaver, 147 – pectoral sandpiper & shrike.

©William Bacon/AlaskaStock.com: pg. 37 – reindeer.

©Jocrebbin/Dreamstime.com: pg. 51 – gray whale.

©Jim Dory: pgs. 1 – girl w/ruff, 14 – king crab, 23 – sow and cubs, 50 – cooking pot & whale, 56 – birders, 58 – long-tailed duck, 60 – loons chasing & fighting, 61 – eagle, 63 – curlew, 64 – sandpiper, 65 – kittiwakes & gull, 68 – swallow, 69 – dipper chicks, 70 – wheatear & buntings, 72 – sparrow, 74 – fish net, 79 – ice fishing, 122 – cormorant, 130 – owl, 131 – sandhill cranes over camps, 136 – shrike, 146 – Front St.

©Patrick Endres/AlaskaPhotographics.com: pgs. 8 – Fox, pg 9 – grebe, 17 – river valley, 27 – gray wolf, 39 – muskox rut, 40 – bear, 42 – lynx & cross fox, 44 – hare, 101 – red fox, 103 – ptarmigan flock, 118 – caribou, 132 – Safety Bridge, 153 – muskox in sunset.

©Carol Gales: pg. 24 – ptarmigan.

©Shane Hertzog: pg. 76 – grayling & Dolly Varden.

©Nick Jans (2011): pgs. 7 – foaming bear, 42 – wolf.

©Jamie Karnik: contents page – shorebird tracks.

©Tom Kohler: pgs. 1 – reindeer, 3 – muskox, 6 – moose, 7 – standing bear, 16 – tundra swans & smelt, 25 – muskox, 26 – plover, 33 – salmon, 34 – moose, 36 – reindeer, 38 – muskox group, 46 – vole, 49 – spotted seal, 54 – bluethroat, 60 – hawk, 63 – semipalmated plover, 69 – warbler & bluethroat, 71 – yellow warbler, 78 – crab, 83 – muskox, 95 – Say's phoebe, 109 – grizzly bear, 121 – cranes, 122 – seal, 124 – loons & pintails, 129 – shoveler & longspur, 130 – muskox, 137 – weasel, 138 – hawk chick, 140 – chickadee.

©John Lane: pg. 104 – moose.

©John McKean: pg. 97 – wagtail.

©Stephan Pietzko/Dreamstime.com: pg. 77 – burbot.

©M. Gordon Sandy: pgs. 52 – killer whale, 57 – dabbling duck.

©Heather Williams/AlaskaStock.com: pg. 5 – muskox and dogs.

©Jim Williams: pgs. 18 – harlequin ducks, 19 – beaver, 46 – muskrat, 54 – swans & eider, 56 – dipper & eagle, 57 – swans & pintail, 58 – eiders, 59 – ptarmigan, 62 – sandhill crane, 63 – golden-plover, 68 – bank swallow nests, 70 – wagtail, 72 – redpoll, 85 – pipit, 102 – wigeon, 125 – godwit, 129 – loon nest, 140 – woodpecker & kingfisher, 141 – moose, 143 – tree swallow, 147 – shoveler, 148 – blackbird & scoters.

Historical photographs

©Anchorage Museum: pg. 36 – Sinrock Mary (Ray B. Dame, Ickes Collection, B1975.175.158).

©University of Alaska Fairbanks: pgs. 92 – walrus hunter (Albert Johnson Collection, UAF-1989-166-402), 98 – Norge (Kay J. Kennedy Aviation Collection, UAF-1962-69-135).

©Alaska State Library: pg. 137 – railway (Alfred G. Simmer, ASL-P137-060).

NOTES

NOTES

NOTES

NOTES

NOTES

NOTES

NOTES

NOTES